Joint Venturing

Joint Venturing

by
Paul W. Beamish

INFORMATION AGE PUBLISHING, INC.
Charlotte, NC • www.infoagepub.com

Library of Congress Cataloging-in-Publication Data

Beamish, Paul W., 1953-
  Joint venturing / by Paul W. Beamish.
     p. cm.
  Includes bibliographical references and index.
  ISBN 978-1-59311-965-2 (pbk.) – ISBN 978-1-59311-966-9 (hbk.)
  1. Joint ventures. I. Title.
  HD62.47.B43 2008
  658'.046–dc22
                                                        2008029426

Copyright © 2008 Information Age Publishing Inc.

All rights reserved. No part of this publication may be reproduced, stored in a retrieval system, or transmitted, in any form or by any means, electronic, mechanical, photocopying, microfilming, recording or otherwise, without written permission from the publisher.

Printed in the United States of America

Contents

Acknowledgments .... *ix*
Preface .... *xi*

PART 1
An Open Mind

1 The Joint Venture Facilitator 3
2 Separating Fact from Fiction 9
3 Before the Joint Venture 15

PART 2
Testing the Strategic Logic

4 Underlying Rationale for Working Together 23
5 The Search for Congruent Measures of Performance 31

PART 3

Partnership and Fit

6	Desire for Stability	41
7	Partner Selection Criteria	47
8	Compatibility	53

PART 4

Shape and Design

9	What Is the Investment Necessary for Success?	63
10	Control and Influence	69
11	Negotiating the Joint Venture	79

PART 5

Operating the JV

12	How Do You Manage Conflict in a JV?	89
13	Learning from IJVs	95
14	Liability of Reorganization	103
15	Intended and Unintended Termination of Joint Ventures	107

PART **6**

I Still Have a Few Questions…

16 Ideal Number of Partners? 117
17 JVs with Small- and Medium-Sized Enterprises (SMEs) 121
18 Licensing As a Non-Equity Alliance 129

Postscript 137
Chapter End Notes 139
Appendix: Case Abstracts 147
Selected Bibliography 163
Index 169

Acknowledgments

For the past twenty-five years, I've been fortunate to learn about joint ventures with and from a large number of joint venture scholars at Ivey and elsewhere. While my own status within this group has evolved from doctoral student to doctoral supervisor, at all times I've tended to view each research or case writing initiative as a true joint exploration.

As the Bibliography at the end of the book suggests, I've engaged in a wide number of joint research projects about joint ventures. In fact many of the chapters in this book are derived from my own joint ventures about joint ventures.

The original core group I learned from and with at Ivey, and with whom I wrote about JVs, included Peter Killing, Harry Lane and Jean Louis Schaan. This was followed (chronologically) by work with Kerry McLellan, Patrick Woodcock, Shige Makino, Andrew Inkpen, Detlev Nitsch, Azimah Ainuddin, Andrew Delios, Carl Fey, Louis Hebert, Kent Neupert, Ruihua Jiang, Iris Berdrow, Charles Dhanaraj, Anthony Goerzen, Ariff Kachra, Chang Choi, Jane Lu, Chris Changwha Chung, and Jing'an Tang. With nearly every one of these scholars, we've worked on multiple projects, and many continue to this day.

Over the years, I've talked with over 500 managers about their joint ventures. A number of the research projects I've undertaken in fact were a result of questions they've asked. I am grateful for their openness as we've jointly pursued answers regarding "what works" and "why."

Joint Venturing, pages ix–x
Copyright © 2008 by Information Age Publishing
All rights of reproduction in any form reserved.

The out-of-pocket expenses to pursue the various joint venture research and case writing initiatives which underpin this book easily run into the hundreds of thousands of dollars. I am grateful to the numerous organizations which have supported this work. Particular thanks are due to SSHRC, and the Ivey PhD program.

Mary Roberts typed and formatted the entire manuscript, and handled all the necessary permissions-to-reprint with her usual good cheer.

A number of people provided comments on earlier drafts, including Nikhil Celly, Kerry McLellan, Jing'an Tang, Jae Jung, Carl Fey, Jason McNicol, and Chris Chung. Thank you.

Notwithstanding the substantial number of people whom I have learned from, all responsibility for any errors or misinterpretations is mine alone.

Preface

This book is written for practicing managers. It is for those who are contemplating the formation of a joint venture and those currently engaged in joint ventures. The book is about best practice: the factors and processes which lead to JV success.

The format of the book is internationally conversational. It follows in the tradition of Russell Robert's fable of free trade and protectionism, *The Choice*, David Chilton's guide to financial planning, *The Wealthy Barber*, and Eli Goldratt's book on global principles of manufacturing, *The Goal*. It uses the Socratic method (question, answer, question, answer) which works so effectively in a case-study classroom. Here the "classroom" is a business-class seat on an international flight.

Underpinning the messages in this book about best practice in JVs is a great deal of research over an extended period of time by a large number of scholars. The sources are contained in the End Notes and Bibliography.

In my experience, practitioners have no real interest in seeing the underlying theory, hypotheses, literature reviews, or statistical analyses. All of these have therefore been eliminated from the main body of the book in order to maintain the desired flow.

Over the years I've been fortunate to be able to (co)author and (co)edit a variety of books, for academics and classroom use. It is fair to say that I have never had as much fun in writing a book as I have with this one. And

I don't think this is solely because I wrote most of it following five years in the Deans' office.

One of the things which is sometimes hard to convey in any book like this is the sheer sense of excitement and achievement that one feels in starting any new business. Joint ventures, when they are working well, can be a source of great satisfaction.

Good luck with your joint venture.

PART 1

An Open Mind

1

The Joint Venture Facilitator

Twenty minutes after the Air Pacific flight had departed, the passengers in the business class section had already been offered drinks, mixed nuts, newspapers, pillows, blankets, travel amenity kits, hangers for their suit coats, menus for the meals to be served over the next 14 hours, deluxe earphones, and instructions on how to operate their personal entertainment systems. For David Lee, in seat 2B, none of these perks relieved at all the growing anxiety he was feeling. Lee was en route to Asia, to hopefully finalize a joint venture agreement he had helped negotiate over the past eleven months. Two parts excited and three parts nervous, Lee couldn't help wonder whether the deal was the right one.

At 44 years of age, Lee had enjoyed a rapid rise within the managerial ranks of the east coast based company he had joined after completing his MBA fifteen years earlier. He had not expected his life to take an international turn—other than for occasional holidays.

Married, with two young children, Lee was as surprised as his wife at how much time he increasingly needed to be away each year on international business trips. "It's where the money is," he had constantly reminded himself and his wife. The night before leaving on this, his third multi-week trip of the past four months, David had had a heated argument with Jill, his wife of 14 years. Now seated with a beer in his hand as the plane hit its cruising altitude of 37,000 feet, David reviewed some of the unsettling comments of the previous evening.

Why do you have to go away again? You just got back!

Like I said, it's where the money is. The economies in Asia are growing a lot faster than ours.

Why don't you send some of your staff?

I would if I could, but this is my deal.

Your deal? What about your family?

You know I don't like being away, but if I can pull this off, I'll have a real shot at the executive VP position in the next few years. Besides I'm not just doing this for me.

So does this mean you'll be away even more?

I don't think so. I think it means I'll have even more control over my schedule.

Do you honestly believe that? Argh. All I can say is that this deal of yours better work, given the price all of us in the family have to pay!

Lovely, thought David. If it isn't enough to have the pressure of trying to get my first joint venture established, up next is jet lag, two weeks of living out of a suitcase as a monk, and the eventual return to a wife who is not pleased. Before David's "happy" thoughts could continue, a voice interjected.

Mr. Lee and, ah, Mr. Boyd, so nice to see you again. I'm Jeffrey, the purser on our flight, and just want you to know I'm here to make your flight as comfortable as possible. Is there anything I can get you right now?

Right. Thanks. *Great.* No, nothing right now.

Hi, since we've been half introduced and we're going to be spending the next half day side by side, let me introduce myself: I'm David Lee.

Peter Boyd here: nice to meet you.

Off to Shanghai for business?

Who isn't these days!

Obviously it's not your first trip.

No, I've been on this flight a "few times" in the past.

Me, this is my third trip in six months. Lately I feel like I ought to be living there, given all the business opportunities. My wife isn't too pleased though.

Ah, so you've joined the model husbands club.

The what?

The model husbands club. Let me explain. A few years ago, I was at a conference. A colleague shared a conversation he'd had with his wife about the lives he, and many of the rest of us, were leading. All of us at this conference were international business professors from university business schools. She'd closed off their conversation by observing that over the years she thought that he had become a model husband. Since he knew she was upset, he gently asked what she meant by that. She said to look it up in the dictionary under model: you know, small imitation of the real thing!

Ouch. That sounds familiar.

Yeah, well there are a couple of dozen guys on every flight who are in that club.

How do you get out?

You don't, at least not while you are building or maintaining an important business.

Can't you use video conferencing, or just go less often?

Sure, and your competitors will go out of their way to remind your mutual customers you're never around, that you are just another of the here today—gone tomorrow types they see so often.

Geez, I was sort of thinking that if I get this deal I've been working on sorted out this trip, I won't have to travel as much.

Well, you could always be the first, David.

So, life must be good at your university if they can afford to fly you business class!

Actually, they aren't the ones paying for this trip. I'm doing a project for a private client.

Hmm. And you teach International Business at your university?

Yes.

I wish now that I'd taken that course when I did my MBA. Seems like my whole life and half our company's profits now come from offshore activity.

Let me guess: you took an extra marketing course instead.

How'd you know? And the thing is, I can't even remember the course.

I've heard this story before.

Ah well.

So, what sorts of things do you teach in international business? A little bit of international finance, a little bit of international operations, a little bit about cultures, . . . ?

Some I.B. professors teach that way. What you've just described is what we call a survey course, an introductory overview of the international aspect of the various functional areas. I actually teach international strategy. This is a course that has two main sections. The first is the internationalization process: setting up exporting arrangements, licensing, joint ventures, your first wholly owned subsidiary. It provides an understanding of the basic modes of involvement, to help know when each is most appropriate. The objective is to demystify international business. The second section deals with managing a multinational enterprise. Here we look at balancing headquarters perspectives, subsidiary perspectives, and country level realities. That sort of thing.

Why didn't I take that course years ago?

Why indeed.

You mentioned that you teach a little bit about joint ventures. I'm actually on my way to China to hopefully establish a joint venture. Can you take a few minutes and tell me what I need to know about setting up joint ventures?

Well, that would take more than a few minutes.

Great, I'm not going anywhere.

But I'm sure you'll want to rest, enjoy the movies. . . .

Actually, I'm not tired at all. Let me buy you a drink Peter.

Drinks are free in business class David.

Yeah, of course. You know what I mean. I'm all ears.

All right, perhaps we can do an abbreviated version of the format I use when I work with companies regarding their joint ventures.

You actually work with companies about their joint ventures?

Yes. That is the reason in fact for the trip I'm on. For much of the past 20 years, I've been studying joint ventures either on my own, or with a large number of talented collaborators. I've also been sometimes working as a joint venture facilitator. The latter is for companies either contemplating the establishment of a JV, or for those already in joint ventures that are struggling.

So a joint venture facilitator tells people what to do about their JVs?

In part, but I actually spend more of the time asking questions. Let me explain it with an analogy. When you purchased your house, did you hire a home inspector before you put your offer in, in order to check to make sure there were no leaks, no water damage, no termites, that it had been build to code, and all that good stuff?

Absolutely, we did it for both houses that we've owned. In fact, we actually had an offer in on one house which the house inspector pointed out was full of problems. The guy we hired spent about four hours at the house, gave us a report, and only charged about $600. Best $600 I ever spent. So, you inspect joint ventures?

What I do is work with the senior management teams of the existing or potential joint venture. I go with the top two to four people from each side, usually to a neutral site, and walk them through a series of questions that ought to be answered regarding every joint venture. It's a form of due diligence. I make a series of short presentations of 20–30 minutes each. Both during and after each presentation, anyone on either side can interrupt, request a break to consult with team members, whatever.... The idea is to make sure the right questions have been asked, and considered, by both partners.

Makes a lot of sense. And you do this in half a day for $600?

No, David. It takes usually 1½–2 days and I charge rather more than $600.

Of course—what am I saying? Sorry about that. So how does it work? And if you don't mind, I think I'll take a few notes.

2

Separating Fact from Fiction

You mentioned that you have a young family, David. I'm a little older than you are so I don't know if parents still read Dr. Spock's classic book, *Baby and Child Care*. For generations of parents, it was the standard for anyone with little ones at home. The first line in that book was both memorable and reassuring to existing and potential parents: "You know more than you think." Well, for the usually younger businesses I work with, international joint ventures, my initial message is less reassuring. Seldom has there been a field of business activity with so much misunderstanding and anecdote masquerading as fact. Unfortunately I'd have to go so far as to conclude that many managers know less about joint ventures than they think!

Oh geez. Why do I think I'm in that category?

A lot of people are, David, which is why the objective of the first of the four stages is in part to separate fact from fiction, to get people to recognize that some of what they think they know as fact about joint ventures is ill founded or unsubstantiated.

Would it surprise you to learn, David, that dozens of business professors around the world actually did their PhD dissertations on the subject of joint ventures, spending years of full time activity developing an understanding of the phenomena? Or that hundreds of refereed articles and hundreds of comprehensive case studies have been written on the subject, and that some of this work is actually pretty insightful?

I had no idea.

What are the sources of information you and your colleagues have used to develop your understanding of joint ventures?

When you pose the question that way, Peter, they actually aren't very good. For myself, it's mostly been newspaper and magazine articles, and a few war stories that one of my colleagues has shared in regards to his experience some years back in a joint venture that failed. Really, it's been pretty hit and miss.

This isn't unusual David. Let's start with the assumptions you have developed about joint ventures. What sort of going-in attitude do you have about joint ventures? Here I'm thinking in terms of such things as profitability, longevity, ease of management, security, and as a corporate priority.

That's easy. First, we view joint ventures as being less profitable then going it alone. Second, we consider joint ventures as a transition—something we tolerate for a while until we can eventually buy out our partner, or perhaps sell out to our partner if things aren't going well. Our impression is that joint ventures don't last as joint ventures, that they all eventually become wholly owned by one of the partners. Third, we have the impression that they are going to be real tough to manage, much tougher than if we owned the investment ourselves. Fourth, we have some serious concerns about using joint ventures out of fear that our partner will steal our technology, and then dump us. And finally, we view JVs as a sort of necessary evil, a mode of investment that is required by law in certain markets.

Well David, this may be a long flight. What if I was to tell you that while all of your concerns "can" happen, in fact most of the time none of them need to happen? In fact, there is a fair bit of available evidence that all five of your views are, how shall I put this, just plain wrong. Allow me to explain.

Before you do that Peter, I think I need another drink.

Let's start with the issue of profitability. Until recently, there wasn't much objective evidence based on large sample sizes or in multiple countries regarding the relative profitability of joint ventures versus wholly owned subsidiaries. For some of the projects I mentioned, I've been working with some colleagues using a massive database on Japanese investments worldwide. It has annual data on the performance of about 30,000 of their subsidiaries around the world. We found that essentially, there is no difference in the overall profitability of joint ventures versus wholly owned subsidiaries.

But is this true for American companies like ours?

It is certainly true for the Japanese-American joint ventures, and joint ventures in virtually every country. Although this is a "Japanese" sample, I think it is significant because it unequivocally shows that JVs don't have to be less profitable.

That's very interesting, Peter. I can use that statistic with my boss.

In terms of stability, the average age of international joint ventures was almost 10 years. This is similar to newly created, wholly owned subsidiaries, or what are sometimes called greenfield investments, and older than acquisitions. Again the key observation here is that JVs can and do survive just as long as wholly owned subsidiaries, which is not really surprising given that they have similar profitability. That said, of course, any company that maintains an attitude or bias that says that JVs just won't last "as" JVs, would typically ensure their bias comes true.

But how stable are joint ventures in absolute terms? I heard somewhere that the failure rate of joint ventures can be just as high as the failure rate of marriages.

Anywhere from one-third to one half of joint ventures will eventually fail, depending on the nationality of the partner. And you're right: they have failure rates that are very similar to those of marriages.

	USA	Japan
Divorces as % of Marriages	50%[a]	25–38%[b]
Joint Venture Exit Rates	50%[c]	33%[d]

Sources:
[a] US Dept. of Health and Human Services, National Center for Health Statistics
[b] Ministry of Health, Labour and Welfare, Japan
[c] Kogut (1988)
[d] Delios and Beamish (2004)

You mentioned that your third concern was that joint ventures were harder to manage. They certainly have a "different" management challenge, given that they require one to coordinate to a greater extent. Some managers get frustrated in JVs by the fact they can't simply mandate or order everyone to do things their preferred way. The flip side of the managerial complexity question is of course that, in a JV, you presumably now have a good partner with some skills and contributions you don't possess.

This ought to make it easier to compete in the market, easing some of the managerial challenge.

You also expressed concern that there is a risk of losing one's technology if the JV does not last. This is a legitimate concern, but one which most companies have been able to overcome. They typically do this via some combination of diligence, introduction of best practice in a staged manner, controlling the technology transfer function themselves in the joint venture, and so forth. Certainly the risk of technology leakage is greater in countries where there is a lack of enforcement of existing intellectual property protection laws. For companies doing business in China for example, there was a large degree of relief with China's admission to the World Trade Organization as this provides a vehicle for greater pressure to be placed on China to respect the intellectual property of others.

Finally, you note that your company's attitude towards JVs was that it was a mode of investment you were forced to use in certain markets. That is really yesterday's news. There was a time that investors were required by many foreign governments to use the JV mode, but this is rarely true nowadays. Even in a market like China which originally required investors to not only use JVs, but expected that the entire investment would revert to China after a certain number of years, they now freely allow wholly owned investments, and don't put any expectations or limits to how long a JV can have a foreign partner. Virtually all countries compete vigorously for foreign investment. There are fewer constraints than ever.

So, if I've got this straight, joint ventures can be just as profitable and survive just as long as wholly owned subsidiaries, they can be managed, they are not a sure way to lose one's technology, and they are entered into voluntarily by lots of firms.

That's it.

Then why do I read so much about the problems with them?

There are a variety of reasons. First of all, bad news sells. A lot of newspapers and magazines seem to focus on the negative. Second, many consultants will emphasize the problems with JVs in order to encourage you to hire them to fix them. Nonetheless, it is a bit of a paradox, isn't it? Anywhere from 25–40% of all foreign investments from all nations take place via joint ventures, yet some people simply don't like them. They find them too messy, with too much uncertainty, and too slow a decision-making process. Interestingly, everyone agrees that they'll be using even more equity joint ventures and non-equity alliances in the future.

Aren't joint ventures and strategic alliances the same thing?

Not exactly. A strategic alliance is a formal, mutually agreed commercial collaboration between companies where the partners pool, exchange or integrate specific business resources, which can affect the long term profitability of the organization. There are innumerable types of strategic alliances. They vary according to the level of interaction required and the level of cooperation—versus competition—inherent in them. Examples of non-equity strategic alliances would include licensing, franchising, R&D consortia, co-production, and so forth. The type of strategic alliance with the greatest requirement for interaction and cooperation is the equity joint venture.

The term strategic alliance has become incredibly over-used in recent years. It is important to recognize that some people use the term very loosely. Some will go so far as to call any longer term business relationship a strategic alliance, not differentiating between what is truly strategic, as opposed to merely important, or ever defining what they mean by an alliance. It's always pretty useful when talking to someone about their strategic alliances to try to determine how inclusive they are being when they use the term.

So, all equity joint ventures are examples of strategic alliances, but not all strategic alliances are joint ventures?

Right.

Wouldn't a company always prefer the equity type of strategic alliance? Wouldn't an equity stake always give them more control over operations, and therefore greater profitability?

Actually, not necessarily. Let me share two examples. You are undoubtedly familiar with IKEA, the giant Swedish furniture retailer. Many years ago, I met with the senior folks in charge of both their Canadian and U.S. operations. I was fascinated at how it was possible for them to construct what appeared to me to be very effective non-equity, buyer-supplier strategic alliances. IKEA had essentially eliminated from the value chain the company that built the furniture. IKEA would instead give component suppliers help with product design, technical assistance, equipment leases, and even lend them money. In turn, the suppliers got new skills, direct access to a growing retailer, and steadier sales. The net result was that IKEA received good quality supply at a lower cost than anyone else. Given my preliminary understanding, I asked the senior people at IKEA North America if I could interview a bunch of their regional suppliers and they said sure. I then arranged some travel funding and was all set to get started when I got a call from an even more senior fellow from IKEA in Europe. It was a short call with what turned out to be the president of IKEA worldwide. He said, "I understand you were planning to do a study of our buyer-supplier relationships because you believe it is the key to our success?" I replied that yes, I was quite excited about working on this project. He then said, in his unforgettable Swedish accent, "Well I can confirm that you are correct. It is the reason we are so successful. However, we don't want you writing about this and telling our competitors how we do it. So, you won't be able to do this study. Have a nice day though." And the phone went dead.

Ouch. That must have hurt.

Now let me contrast that with the experience of Kentucky Fried Chicken when they entered China. As you may recall, they were the first major western fast food company to set up in the People's Republic. In fact, their first restaurant was a modest little affair—it seated 500 people—in an obscure location, on the edge of some place called Tiananmen Square in Beijing. Yet even though they were an early entrant, with a great product for that market, their original joint venture faltered. They ran into problems with redundant partner contributions, misunderstanding of the JV agreement by the local partner, senior management changes, and diverging performance measures. Eventually, they had to set up an entirely different joint venture arrangement, which only then allowed them to grow dramatically.

My point of these two examples is that equity is not necessarily preferable to non-equity, and going first is not a guarantee of success.

3

Before the Joint Venture

So *Peter, are we ready to talk about how to design a successful joint venture and more particularly my joint venture?*

Almost. But before we get into the specifics of testing the strategic logic, partnership and fit, and shape and design, we ought to back up for a few minutes and consider a few pre-JV issues.

The first of these relates to why you and your company are even thinking of increasing your actual number of foreign investments. Would it make sense for you to instead expand one of your existing operations? As you know, every time a company establishes a new subsidiary, whether wholly or partially owned, there are a bunch of one-time and ongoing details that have to be dealt with. For some organizations, once everything is factored in, it's easier to simply grow the scale of a subsidiary that is already in place.

Sometimes the decision rules, which guided the establishment of previous subsidiaries, may not apply any longer. For example, there may now be different applicable tax rates, shipping times, shipping costs, quality levels possible, intellectual property protection realities, and so on. Did you guys spend much time on this?

Actually, here's an area where we really did do our homework. We looked at the issue from a variety of perspectives. We considered whether there were manufacturing economies of scale from growing an existing business, the cost/benefits from exporting from multiple sites, and so on. We even had one of our most technology oriented junior staff do some modeling. So, we feel pretty comfortable with this.

Excellent. Given that, the next obvious question is why go to this particular market? One of the great growth industries of the past 50 years has been map making. I'm a long time subscriber to the annual edition of The Atlas of Global Development, or what used to be called The World Bank Atlas. In the past 20 years alone, the number of countries in the atlas has grown from 184 to 208! That's 24 new countries! So, every company has lots of choices in regards to candidate countries for investment. While there is intense competition among countries to attract foreign investment, typically only a small number are ever seriously considered for any company's investment. A lot of otherwise capable executives have a pretty underdeveloped awareness of market sizes. Let me illustrate. I've been using this simple exercise with my MBA students for years. They are a cocky group and it helps them learn a little humility. Let me pull it up on my laptop. Here it is. I ask students to fill in the names of the 12 largest countries in the world against the actual figures for population, gross national income, and gross national income measured by purchasing power parity. I promise to buy dinner at the restaurant of their choosing for anyone who gets it right. Anyways, I've never come close to having to pay out, despite using the exercise with over 1,000 people.

Oh yeah? Let me have a look.

Sure. Take your time.

Oh nuts. Once I get past China, India, America, Russia, and Japan on the population list, I don't know. And once I get past the G7 on GNI, I'm not sure either. And purchasing power parity, I've never even thought about that. Better, make it 1001 people you haven't had to buy dinner for!

There is obviously a lot more to market selection than population and wealth, but I'm sure you'll agree, a basic understanding of global demographics isn't a bad starting point.

Makes sense.

So how many countries did your company seriously consider investing in?

One. We felt we absolutely had to be in China. Everybody else had either already set up there or was in the process of doing so, and we didn't want to be left behind.

There's no question that China has been attracting a phenomenal amount of FDI, and a lot of firms feel the same as you do. Did you go there because it was a low cost manufacturing and/or because it was an important market?

Cheap labor was our objective. We don't really know how big the market in China is, or will be, for our product.

Top Twelve Rankings

	Purchasing Power Parity GDP[a] (Int'l $ Billion) Economic output measured by looking at the prices of a bundle of goods and services at home in local currencies	**Gross National Income[b] (GNI) (in U.S. $ Billion)** Economic output measured by valuing each country's goods and services in dollars, using three year average exchange rates	**Population[b] (Million)**
1	12,970	12,970	1,305
2	10,000	4,988	1,095
3	4,220	2,852	297
4	4,042	2,264	220
5	2,585	2,263	186
6	1,903	2,178	156
7	1,871	1,724	143
8	1,727	1,100	142
9	1,723	1,052	132
10	1,616	793	128
11	1,180	765	103
12	1,165	753	83

[a] *Source*: The World Fact Book as at March 15/07; most are estimates for 2006.
[b] *Source*: 2007 Atlas of Global Development; figures for 2005.

Well the good news for you is that China is rapidly becoming a major purchaser of higher end goods and services from lots of countries. That said, as with every other country, there are some things that can be particularly worrisome regarding investment there. Did you give much thought to where you might invest next if it wasn't China? Or, What the showstoppers might be in regards to investing there?

Like I said, we pretty much decided China was it, and didn't think about alternatives. And in terms of showstoppers, our attitude was that if it's good enough for everybody else, it's good enough for us. I hate to ask, but are there some things you think we should be concerned about regarding investing in China?

Every country has things which investors should be concerned about. And the lists don't stay constant. In the case of China, it would include threat of currency revaluation, lack of intellectual property protection enforcement, corruption, the Taiwan issue, and so on. Don't get me wrong; I'm not suggesting for a moment that you don't invest. In fact there are lots of sound reasons for making foreign investments, both in general, and specifically in China. All I'm suggesting is that it's a good idea to either reserve some time yourself, or charge someone with the responsibility, to keep abreast of the changing environment. I've been going to China every year since the early 1980s and every five years or so I conclude that the China I used to know well is now a new place.

Doesn't sound like I'll be doing less traveling any time soon. (Maybe my wife was right, again: I have been kidding myself.)

You mentioned that there were three things we should talk about in the pre-JV stage. What's the third?

Timing. Essentially, it's why invest now? You've addressed this already in part but it's useful to underscore both the why-now and the for-how-long questions. Some companies try to be the first one into a market because they figure first mover advantages will exceed first mover disadvantages. Others are fast followers. Then there is the herd, which is where your company seems to be at, and then there are the real laggards and no-gos.

That sounds accurate. One of the senior guys in our company had been beating the drum for years about the need for us to get more internationally oriented but most of the senior management then was not interested. Business was "good enough" at home, without the hassle of going international.

What changed?

What didn't! We got a new CEO and he wasn't satisfied with "good enough." A lot of the senior managers, who were indifferent or complacent about the advantages of going international, were moved out of the company. Our new CEO emphasized the need for us to be less ethnocentric because we'd make more money that way. He said we needed to build a group of geocentric managers.

Well he's certainly right. No question that people have to have the right mindset, one which embraces the opportunities which exist elsewhere, if they want to improve their chances of success and their profitability. But even the right mindset isn't enough if there isn't a clear sense of why we're doing the investment now, and how long we expect it to last.

We are pretty comfortable with why we are doing it now. In terms of our expectations of how long it will last, well, we sort of expect it to be permanent.

But didn't you say you were going there in part because of low-cost labor? What will you do when labor costs get too high there? You'll recall that a lot of jobs in North America moved to the maquiladoras in Mexico when NAFTA was signed. I was in Mexico recently, and some of those factories are now being moved to Asia. My point is that it's useful to carefully lay out the assumptions—financial and otherwise—underlying why you are going now, and what might have to change for you to modify your thinking. At a minimum your successor will thank you for providing some institutional memory.

Fair enough.

So, can we talk about my joint venture now?

Sure, but let's first have dinner. And I wouldn't mind a glass of that Ebenezer Shiraz they are offering from Australia's Barossa Valley.

PART 2
Testing the Strategic Logic

4

Underlying Rationale for Working Together

O*kay Peter, I think I now have a more open mind about joint ventures. So what do we start with?*

The strategic logic. We need to resolve a series of questions. All are necessary but not sufficient conditions for proceeding. If they can be satisfactorily resolved, we can then go on to discussion of partnership and fit, and shape and design.

But what if we can't resolve the questions you are going to ask? What if there is fundamental disagreement either within the company or with our proposed partner about what we ought to do?

The short answer is that you better think long and hard about whether to proceed. Joint ventures require a strong foundation. We've all read the horror stories about buildings that suddenly collapse, killing people and causing millions of dollars of damage. The subsequent investigations usually uncover some combination of poor engineering; the use of building materials that weren't up to code, or some such. Well, while a failed joint venture won't physically kill someone, it sure can kill some careers. And it certainly can easily cause millions of dollars in losses, and lost opportunities.

Fair enough. But surely you are always going to have "some" reservations about proceeding with any joint venture?

Of course, but the point is you want to go into this with your eyes wide open, with a more complete awareness of where the inevitable difficulties may lie.

Got it. So how do we test the strategic logic?

We start by asking why we are discussing working together. In every joint venture, there first has to be an underlying rationale that leads us to conclude that the equity joint venture organization form makes more sense than any of the other alternative alliance or investment forms. Second, we—and our partner—have to believe that we'll be able to resolve the predictable trouble spots that arise. Let's look at some examples. Give me a second while I turn on my laptop again since I have a few graphics.

The first example starts by looking at the underlying reasons for working together, in terms of products and markets. Take a minute and look over this simple 2 × 2 matrix on the Motives for Joint Venture Formation. It isn't intended to be an exhaustive list of reasons for joint venturing, just the most frequently observed rationales.

Anything on it that is unclear?

No, this seems pretty straightforward. The only point I'm not so clear about is in regards to "co-opting a competitor." Isn't it sometimes illegal to join forces with a competitor?

Ah, I suspect you are thinking of anti-trust and restraint of trade laws. For well over 99% of all joint ventures, especially the international ones, this is not a real issue. The reason it isn't an issue is that in the international market, you typically have lots and lots of existing and potential competitors.

Now allow me to continue.

The most typical type of joint venture, at least from an international perspective, is the taking of existing products (for sale and/or manufacturing purposes) to a new national market. The second most commonly observed type is to acquire foreign products for the existing, local market(s).

Underlying Rationale for Working Together ■ 25

In both of these traditional types, one partner will usually provide the technology/brand while the other will provide market knowledge.

That's exactly why we are doing our JV.

Motives for Joint Venture Formation

	Existing Products	**New Products**
Existing markets	*Purpose*: to strengthen the existing business	*Purpose*: to acquire new products for existing markets (product diversification)
	Why Use a JV: • create economies of scale • reduce financial risk • acquire new skills/capabilities • co-opt a competitor • save time	Why Use a JV: • create economies of scope • less expensive than an acquisition • more help then a license arrangement • faster and surer then developing a new product internally
New markets	*Purpose*: to take existing products to new markets (market diversification)	*Purpose*: to enter a new business (product *and* market diversification)
	Why Use a JV: • to gain access to (a partner's) knowledge of the local economy, politics and culture • acquisitions may be too expensive or uncertain • quicker and surer market penetration approach than going alone • local government investment incentives	Why Use a JV: • unrelated acquisitions have higher failure rate • faster than doing it alone • share costs • spread the (higher) risks associated with this level of uncertainty

Now, I've got another graphic here somewhere that illustrates this, and also talks about some of the issues associated with it. Every alliance and investment type has its issues: strengths and weaknesses, advantages and limitations. More importantly, we pretty much know what these are before we start. Take this example:

Example 1

Equity JVs: To take existing products to new markets
or acquire foreign products for local markets

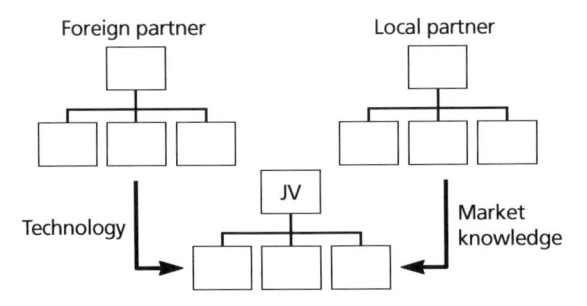

```
   Foreign partner              Local partner
        ▢                            ▢
   ┌────┼────┐                  ┌────┼────┐
   ▢    ▢    ▢                  ▢    ▢    ▢
                    JV
   Technology ┐    ▢    ┌ Market
              │   ┌┴┐   │ knowledge
              └──▶▢ ▢◀──┘
```

- Issues
   - role of each partner in management of venture
   - transfer prices
   - "fairness" of technology and management payments
   - stability of JV: varies according to type of contribution

The most common issues in traditional product or market diversification joint ventures relate to (a) the role of each partner in the management of the venture; (b) transfer prices for the inputs to, and output of, the venture, i.e., in which country do you book the profits; (c) stability, which I'll talk more about later; and (d) the "fairness" of certain technology and management fees.

Allow me to share a story in regards to this last point. When I first started investigating issues around joint venture performance nearly 25 years ago, I went looking for a context where I thought there'd likely be significant cultural differences between the partners. The closest emerging markets to where I lived were in the Caribbean and Mexico. Since my Spanish language abilities didn't go much beyond "*dos cervacas por favor,*" I chose the English-speaking Caribbean.

And I suppose you visited the islands during your winter?

That was just a coincidence, honest. Anyways, the joint ventures I looked at had an ABC partner (American, British, or Canadian) and a local partner in Jamaica, Barbados or one of the other islands. In order to understand what was really going on in the joint ventures there, I had this policy of talking to both partners. The reason I wanted to talk to both partners was a concern that I might not get the whole story by just talking to one.

Makes sense.

So, one day for one of these joint ventures, I got the foreign company perspective from the joint venture general manager in the morning, and the local company perspective in the afternoon. I started in the morning interview with an open-ended question: How's your joint venture doing?

"Fantastic," the general manager said. "Our company has five joint ventures around the world and this one is the best performer of the bunch."

"Why is that?" I asked.

"We structured it so that it generates multiple sources of income. We are earning a 5% technology transfer fee, a 6% management fee, and some licensing royalties. Plus the joint venture itself is throwing off a small profit."

"Sounds great," I said. "How does the future look?"

"Fantastic."

About three hours later, I'm sitting down with the local partner, the patriarch of a well-known, diversified group of local firms. After the usual introductions, I start with the same open-ended question: "How's your joint venture doing?"

"Terrible," he says. "One of the worst businesses we've ever participated in. Our partner seems to like it, but all we earn from it is about a 2% return. We'd have been better off leaving our money in a savings account in the bank."

"How does the future of it look?" I asked.

"Terrible," he says. "I'll be surprised if the joint venture still exists in six months time."

Well that joint venture didn't even last another three months. Was this a predictable problem area in traditional joint ventures, one that should have been attended to much earlier in the process? Absolutely.

Let me quickly share a second and third example, just to reinforce this point.

Lots of joint ventures are set up, as you know, for supply purposes. For example, auto parts companies might join together to produce a part that they each need. They join together in order to achieve economies of scale.

Example 2
Equity JVs: To supply your own firm...

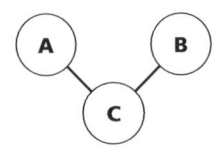

- **C** has the potential for economies of scale in:
  - research and development
  - purchasing
  - manufacturing
- **C** may also reduce uncertainty of supply
- Issues
  - ownership proportions versus volumes
  - where to capture the profit
  - design of the **C** product

Just like with every other JV type, there are some typical issues that arise. Here they relate to (a) whether it is possible to align one's equity holdings in the joint venture with the venture's production output used by that partner; (b) where to capture the profit—the JV or at the parent company level; (c) the design of the product being produced by the joint venture. It isn't usually a problem at the start, but can become one later on when respective needs evolve.

I can see how these could become pretty sticky issues. So I guess you just hope for the best, that you can resolve them when and if they arise, right?

No. What I think makes more sense is to discuss them when it isn't yet a real problem, when people are not yet entrenched, when you can have an adult discussion on guiding principles. Let me show you a third example that might clarify this.

Example 3
Equity JVs: Functional area (i.e., R & D)

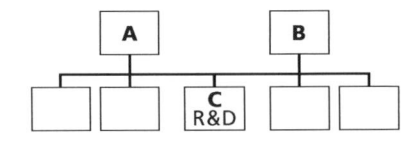

  - a new R & D unit is formed which employs researchers from both (all) partners
- Issues
  - the fact the two parents may be competitors
  - the risk of organizational problems
  - which R & D people get sent?

Typical issues in this particular type of functional area joint venture include (a) the fact that sometimes the two parents are still competitors, so wonder whether all technical advances will in fact equally flow back to both? (b) conversely, the risk of organizational problems resulting from the fact that scientists sometimes feel a greater loyalty to their discipline than to their company. Will they forget who provided them to the joint venture? (c) questions around whether each partner will send their best people to the JV, or their second team in hopes that their partner will send their best people?

Nobody would actually do that would they?

They have. They do. They will. This is why it's so useful to discuss these issues before they happen, in hopes that this will prevent them from ever occurring. Fortunately most firms don't try to play games with their partners, but enough have in the past that it is worth developing a few protocols up front.

Right.

So to recap. The first part of testing the strategic logic focuses on getting to a clear understanding of why the organizations are proposing to work together. Clear, significant benefits have to exist for each partner. It has to be win-win. There also has to be a sense that whatever type of equity joint venture organization form is chosen, it is superior to the available alternatives, even though it inevitably has its own limitations. And finally, the partners expect to be able to work through the predictable trouble spots.

This makes sense. But I do have one question. What if there is a strong, strategic logic, but it's a short-term logic? What if we only need a partner for a few years?

Then you likely shouldn't use the equity joint venture form. Or if you are using it, you need to be up-front with your partner. The equity joint venture form is best used when one really does need a partner, and not just for a temporary period or problem.

5

The Search for Congruent Measures of Performance

A major issue in the discussion of strategic logic is to determine whether congruent measures of performance exist between the partners.

But, Peter, surely this is an obvious one. Both simply want to make money.

That's it? That's the only way success is measured in your company? I suspect your planning and budgeting processes are rather more detailed than that.

Well sure. They consider return on equity, return on sales, return on assets, EBITDA (earnings before interest, taxes, depreciation, and amortization)...

What about growth? Market share? Stock market reaction? Managerial satisfaction and morale?

Yeah okay, those all matter to varying extents, depending on who you are talking to in the company.

What about the stability of the business? Some people view the noise level present in a business as a success measure. They feel that too many organization changes, especially abrupt or unplanned ones, can reflect badly on the firm.

All right, let me raise the white flag of surrender on this one. When I actually think about it, there are dozens of ways of measuring success, and they certainly are sometimes at odds with each other.

Exactly, and as we'll discuss in a few minutes, this issue gets more complicated in joint ventures.

Lovely. Maybe I need another drink.

Perhaps you'll want to wait a few minutes on that. If you remember nothing else from our conversation today, I hope it's what I'm going to share next! Allow me to explain this with a stylized example of a joint venture and with a story.

Sure, please go ahead. I shouldn't consume so much alcohol on these flights anyways. You have some drinks, it makes you dehydrated. Then you drink some more. Then you've got to keep using the washroom, then....

Back to our joint venture, David.... In every joint venture, there are at least three perspectives that matter—those of the two partners (assuming it is only two partners) and that of the joint venture general manager (JVGM).

Let's start with the foreign partner's perspective. The foreign partner, when asked about how he or she will measure performance, may quite explicitly say something along the lines of: we want profits. Say 20% return on sales, within 12–24 months after investing. And if pushed slightly, he or she might add—and we don't want to chew up a huge amount of senior management time in overseeing the JV.

Well, there are two problems already. The first is that the two explicit measures are not necessarily internally consistent. The company wants healthy and fast profitability from the JV, but doesn't want to devote much time to it.

Second, like every other firm, they actually have some implicit performance measures, or if not measures, at least assumptions. These latter measures or assumptions are so obvious to anyone in the company, that it doesn't even occur to them to discuss them with their partner. These are below the dotted line in my graphic. In the first of these, they want to maximize local sales, since after all, they want to keep their options open in regards to setting up JVs in other neighboring countries. The second implicit point is that they want to use their existing or mature (or maybe even peripheral) technology, in hopes that they can squeeze out even a greater return on their previous investment in R&D, plus eliminate the possibility of losing their current technology, should the JV not work out.

Got it. Problems of internal consistency and problems of explicit versus implicit.

The Search for Congruent Measures of Performance ■ 33

Measuring JV performance
The search for congruity

Foreign partner
i.e., 1. Profitability—20% ROS (within 12–24 months)
2. Require limited senior management time
----
3. Maximize local sales
4. Exploit peripheral or mature technology

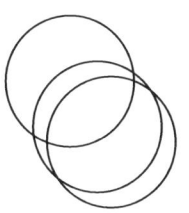

Now let's turn to the local partner perspective. The local partner, when asked about how he or she will measure performance, may quite explicitly say: we want profits. And we want them pretty soon—say 9–12 months, since we don't have as deep pockets as our partner. And if pushed slightly, he or she might add—and we would hope that there would be some good paying salaries available to us within the joint venture.

Once again, there are two problems already. The first is that again the two explicit measures are not internally consistent. The local partner wants fast profitability but also high paying salaries for him and perhaps some of his associates. Second, they too have some implicit assumptions that are so obvious to them that they don't even think to discuss them with the foreign partner. The first of these is that they want to be able to export to other countries out of the new joint ventures. After all, why would anyone want territorial constraints? Second, they want the newest technology, the current technology, and the best possible technology. Their approach is along the lines of "why would anyone want to learn how to make rotary telephones in a digital world?" They want every chance to succeed in the future, and have a legitimate concern that yesterday's technology may not allow them to compete very well or for very long.

Measuring JV performance
The search for congruity

Local partner
i.e., 1. Profitability (within 9–12 months)
2. High paying salaried positions
----
3. Opportunity to export
4. Obtain newest technology

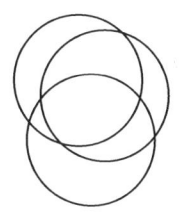

So, same sort of issue, but within each partner.

Right. And it gets even more complicated then that. Let me share a story now with you.

When I conduct the various joint venture facilitations, I always ask the executives present to go through a short exercise. I ask everyone to write down on a sheet of paper the three main ways in which they think the performance of the JV should be measured. I explain that I'm going to ask each person to share their top three only with the other people present from their company. Further, I explain that at the end of the first part of the exercise, before we discuss anything between the partners, everyone should feel free to suggest a short recess, if desired.

Now at this point, I almost inevitably get a raised-eyebrow look from one or both of the presidents. It is a look that says, "Why are we wasting time with anything so obvious? My senior management team and I worked this out months ago." When I get "the look," I ask them to humor me, and to please go ahead and jot down their top three measures of performance for the proposed joint venture.

So, they humor me. They take a few minutes, and write down their measures. Then I exchange the respective lists with those of other people within their firm. Then the fun starts.

Each person quickly scans someone else's list. Then they look at the person. Then they look at the list again. And then within a minute, somebody says "Maybe this would be a good time for a short break" and somebody from the other partner team says, "Yes, that sounds like a good idea to me."

So then each team returns to one of the breakout rooms we have available. I go back and forth between the rooms, observing.

In all the years I've been doing these joint venture facilitations, never once have the senior management teams of any of the partner groups, agreed on their top three measures.

Not once?

Not once. And again, we aren't talking about between the partners—we are talking about within each parent company.

Oh wow. So, there is usually a break at this point?

There is always a break at this point. And in the respective breakout rooms, there is sometimes some pretty heated internal discussions. All of the executives present are savvy enough to recognize that they can't expect to discuss performance objectives with a potential partner if they haven't already got crystal clear internally agreed measures.

The Search for Congruent Measures of Performance ▪ **35**

So, I imagine that these "short recesses" may sometimes not be so short.

Most go 15–30 minutes, but one stretched for nearly two hours.

The other partner must have been pretty irked at being left sitting there for so long.

Actually no. He quite rightly thought there would be big advantages to him if he knew exactly how his potential partner was planning to measure success.

I can see that now.

What about that third perspective you mentioned—the joint venture general manager's?

Right.

If you ever meet any joint venture general managers, be nice to them. They have a tough job. I remember talking to the Singapore-born store manager of KFC's first restaurant in China, soon after it opened. He explained that he "only" had two problems: all his customers and all his employees!

When you ask joint venture general managers how they measure success, they typically provide three responses.

Measuring JV performance
The search for congruity

The JV General Manager
i.e., 1. Profitability as soon as possible
2. Avoid bad relationships between partners
3. Look at exporting/technology issue in terms of Return on Sales

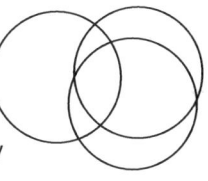

The first is, they want profitability as soon as possible. The sooner the joint venture is generating a profit, the sooner both partners stop looking over his or her shoulder at every decision being taken. Their second measure of success is "avoiding bad relationships" between the partners. Essentially they want the partners to not be fighting. If the partners are fighting, it's right through the JVGM. Not a place you want to be. Their third measure is in relation to the local sales versus export, and new versus old technology questions. They simply ask: "What is best for the joint venture?" JVGMs hope that when their performance is being evaluated, that both partners will agree that he or she put the performance of the joint venture first.

Peter: You've painted a picture that can be pretty scary. How do you ever get perfect congruity?

Measuring JV performance
The search for congruity

Foreign partner
i.e., 1. Profitability—20% ROS (within 12–24 months)
2. Require limited senior management time
- -
3. Maximize local sales
4. Exploit peripheral or mature technology

Local partner
i.e., 1. Profitability (within 9–12 months)
2. High paying salaried positions
- -
3. Opportunity to export
4. Obtain newest technology

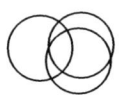

The JV
i.e., 1. Profitability as soon as possible
2. Avoid bad relationships between partners
3. Look at exporting/technology issue in terms of Return on Sales

You don't. Joint ventures aren't a world of make believe. Partners will have different objectives, and for legitimate reasons. You'll never get perfect congruity.

What you can realistically aim for, however, is strongly overlapping measures of success. The process of teasing out what really matters to each partner can also provide insight with respect to reactions one can expect from your partner to actions that might occur when the JV is operational.

If you can't achieve strongly overlapping performance measures in the negotiation process, it should serve as a giant warning bell, one that screams out: "Proceed with extreme caution." Now, most organizations are able to agree on the importance of performance measures that are pretty congruent. They recognize that getting an organization, joint venture or otherwise, all pulling in the same direction can be a powerful (and profitable) force.

How do you increase the likelihood of everyone associated with the JV pulling in the same direction?

Five ways. The first starts with you. How exactly do you think performance should be measured, and why? It's worth the time to list out the performance measures considered and why you do, or don't, propose to use them.

Second, ask your colleagues to do the same thing. Often times the subsequent discussion leads to an internal debate. This is healthy. It is not reasonable to ask any partner to try to respond to mixed corporate messages depending on whom from your company they happen to meet with on any given day.

Third, ask your partners to consider following a similar process. Most will appreciate and value the care you are taking to get this right.

Fourth, if it is an already established joint venture, don't forget the general manager. This is the person who lives with the business every day.

Finally, keep asking. Technologies change. Competitive environments change. Senior managers change. Consequently, desired performance measures can evolve.

PART 3

Partnership and Fit

6

Desire for Stability

David: The good news is that a sound strategic logic will take you a long way towards joint venture success. The bad news is that it won't take you all the way. Ensuring that a sound strategic logic exists for any joint venture is a necessary but still not sufficient condition for overall success. The next stage for any organization that is joint venturing is partnership and fit.

Before we talk about that Peter, I have to say that I'm feeling a lot better about my joint venture. I was mentally applying the points you were raising to my situation, and at least for many of them, I think I'm in reasonable shape. For some of the other points, well, I've got some new agenda items for the next meeting with our partner.

Excellent. Glad to hear it.

Any discussion of partnership and fit can naturally fall into three sections. The first of these relates to what you want from a partner, while the other two are elements of the partner selection process.

Virtually every organization engaged in a joint venture wants something from its partner: otherwise, they wouldn't use that organization form. Each partner has knowledge of something not possessed by the other partner, which can strengthen the overall enterprise.

Yet the partner knowledge being sought has to be placed in a particular context. Specifically, most organizations which enter into joint ventures want the actual joint venture to survive, and ideally along the way to be stable.

Doesn't everyone want his or her joint venture to survive, and to be stable?

Actually no. Some folks will have a different motivation and not have the same longer-term orientation you have. It's for that reason we need to ensure that there is a fit between what we want from our partner, and what our partner wants from us.

So how can you determine if such a fit exists?

For me, stability comes down to whether each partner is satisfied with the fact the other partner is fully contributing its unique knowledge, skills, clients, relationships and markets to the joint venture, versus whether it feels compelled to actually acquire what its partner knows. Let me try and illustrate this with a graphic.

	Parent A	
What do you want from your partner?	**Wants access to partner's knowledge**	**Wants acquisition of partner's knowledge**
Parent B — Wants access to partner's knowledge	*The classic "joint" venture* • A cooperative alliance (very stable)	*Mixed motive* • A pseudo alliance (eventually unstable)
Parent B — Wants acquisition of partner's knowledge	*Mixed motive* • A pseudo alliance (eventually unstable)	*"Race to learn"* • A competitive alliance (very unstable)

In the first scenario, the joint venture is able to fully access the knowledge and skills of each partner. Neither partner is trying to acquire what the other knows. Each partner is satisfied with access. This is the classic or traditional joint venture. It tends to be very stable.

In the second scenario, one of the two partners is not satisfied with the joint venture merely having access to its partner's knowledge. Instead they want to acquire what the partner knows. Not surprisingly, this mixed-motive joint venture is eventually unstable. Once the partner who wanted to acquire the other partner's knowledge gets enough of what they want, they'll find a way to dissolve the joint venture.

There is a third scenario, but it is unusual. Here, both partners make no secret of the fact that they are only in the joint venture long enough to figure out how to acquire what the other knows. This is a competitive joint venture, if that doesn't sound like an oxymoron. It is very unstable. It won't survive. But because the terms are acceptable to both partners going in, sort of like consenting adults, it can't be considered a failure or unsuccessful when it is eventually closed or sold to one of the partners.

So it's really the second scenario that is the problem.

Right.

So why don't all partners try to acquire what the other knows?

For quite a few reasons, actually. First, the cost of obtaining it may exceed the pay off. It could be too expensive or time consuming, given the potential returns. Second, there may be a recognition that the partner will always be stronger in its contribution than we could ever realistically hope to be. The partner may own advantages that are too tough to duplicate. Third, it may lack the necessary skills to acquire the knowledge. These skills can range from technical skills, to language skills, to a supporting infrastructure. Fourth, it will have other priorities. It makes no sense for any firm to try and know everything about every business in every country. Companies focus on the development of core skills for good reasons. Thus for example, a firm may be far better off in allocating its limited managerial resources to the development of a series of joint ventures that will allow it to exploit its current technical advantage, then it will by trying to personally learn all the intricacies of doing business in a particular country.

This makes sense. What I'm still unclear about though is how you can tell whether I am getting a partner who wants to acquire what I know, as opposed to being satisfied that I'm giving the JV access to my contributions?

Good question. And I don't have a great answer because, after all, the partner who wants to acquire may not be telling you what they are up to.

But that's my point. Isn't there any way of telling?

There are a few. First, you can and should directly ask your potential partner about their motivations. At a minimum, it will clarify expectations. Second, you can look at, or ask your potential partner about, their track record with joint ventures. Have they had a bunch of short-lived ones? Third, for an existing joint venture, you can watch to see if excessive numbers of expatriates are being assigned to the joint venture, or conversely if requests for technical information go beyond operational needs.

44 ▪ Joint Venturing

Peter: You've been talking about the importance of the two partners clarifying what each wants from the other, in order to ensure survival and stability. I get the impression though that you are typically assuming a partnership of equals.

That's right.

But not all joint ventures seem to have a roughly even split between the partners' equity holdings. Does the amount of equity each partner holds influence the survival of the joint venture? It seems to me that I'd be more committed to any joint venture that I had a real stake in. My boss talks about the need for us to have some skin in the game.

David, your instincts are pretty good on this point. While it is not exactly a straight-line relationship between equity and survival, it does go in that direction. When one has a very small stake in a joint venture, say 20% or less, the mortality risk is two to four times as great as a wholly owned subsidiary. In Figure 6.1 the mortality risk for wholly owned subsidiaries is shown as the base case, that is, as 1. However, by the time one gets to a 40% equity stake, the mortality risk is little different than that of wholly owned subsidiaries.

So basically this seems to tell me that once you have a certain minimum percentage of the equity in an investment, you treat it just as seriously as you would any subsidiary you wholly owned, and by doing so, a higher likelihood of survival will result.

Yes, I think that's a fair summary.

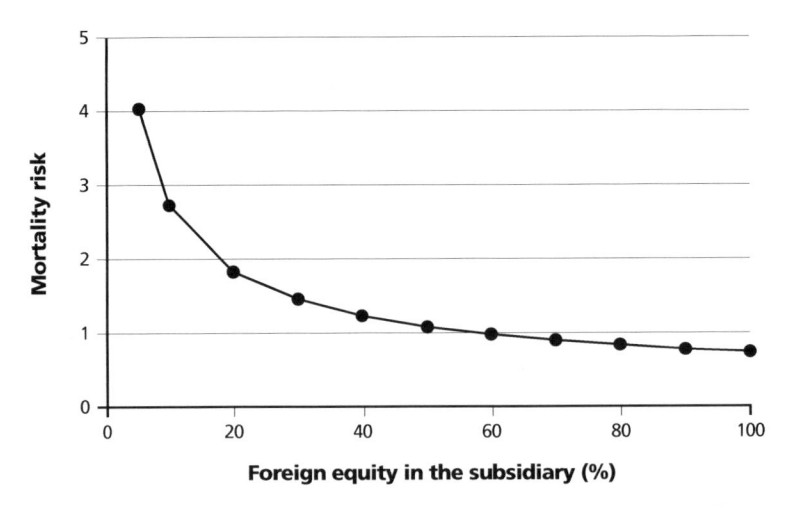

Figure 6.1 Effect of equity on mortality risk. *Note:* 1 = equivalent to wholly owned subsidiary.

Will the ideal amount of equity be the same no matter where you are investing? I guess what I'm thinking is that it is easier for us to invest in a place like Canada than in a place like China. They speak the same language in Canada as we do in America, they are right next-door, and we've gotten to know their market pretty well over the years. In contrast, China is "foreign."

David, this is an excellent question, one which international business researchers have been grappling with for some time. One stream of research argues that multinational corporations will want to *increase* their level of control when there is a large cultural distance between you and the country you are investing in. The implicit, underlying assumption here is that higher equity control will be necessary because cultural distance and managing costs will increase in tandem.

In contrast, a second stream of research links increases in cultural distance with the *loosening of control* as a way to reduce uncertainty and information costs. This perspective argues that you don't want to take a high equity control stance in markets that you don't understand.

So which one is right?

Actually, there is a way to reconcile the two views, essentially by focusing on the age of the investment. Subsidiary age moderates the effects of cultural distance on equity control issues. When a firm initially enters a foreign market, cultural distance plays a role. However, as the firm adjusts to the foreign market, the importance of cultural distance decreases and at some point ceases to play much of a role in the firm's strategies. In essence the influence of national cultural distance is temporary.

As can be seen from Figure 6.2, cultural distance has a significantly greater impact on ownership levels for newer subsidiaries than for older subsidiaries. The effect of cultural distance diminishes with subsidiary age. MNCs may even slightly loosen ownership control on their subsidiaries over time as they learn to adapt to the host country environment.

Okay, I can see why that would be so, but what is the implication for me?

In strategic terms it suggests that when subsidiaries are located in culturally distant markets, many executives are more inclined toward higher equity control during the early stages of operations. Managers may then plan for a loosening of equity control as the firm gains greater knowledge and experience in those markets. Because the perceived need for greater equity control diminishes over time, joint ventures, strategic alliances, the use of distributors and other low control modes become increasingly viable. Similarly, the need for highly skilled expatriate managers should diminish as firms gain knowledge and experience in particular country markets. This

46 ■ *Joint Venturing*

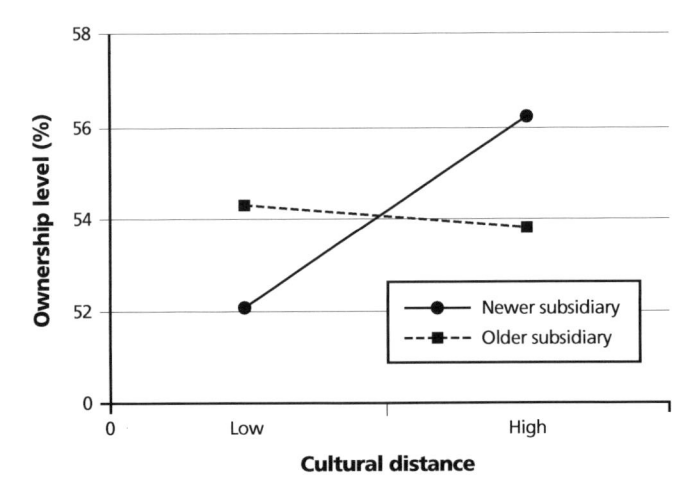

Figure 6.2 The interaction effect between subsidiary age and cultural distance on ownership level.

is good news for firms struggling with the high cost of fielding expatriate managers. So, the knowledge that the negative effects stemming from cultural distance are likely to be temporary should provide you with greater flexibility as you make entry and operational mode decisions.

7

Partner Selection Criteria

So, if we get the equity level right, does this mean we can spend less time on finding the right partner?

No. Identifying and selecting a partner is among the most important considerations in establishing a joint venture. It also may be the most difficult and time-consuming. Even though partner selection can be the determining factor in success or failure, it is often not given the time and attention that it deserves.

But isn't the partner the source of most problems in JVs?

The most common problems cited with joint ventures certainly involve the partner. However, it is far too easy to automatically blame one's partner when conflict arises, too easy to blame the other guy, and not to question one's own contribution to the problem.

So how does one evaluate a potential partner?

At least three main questions have to be asked: Does the partner possess the skills I need? Will I get access? Will we be compatible?

Those sound like pretty sensible questions, but it also sounds like it might take a while to do the necessary due diligence. Is there any short cut possible?

Many firms are impatient to find a partner in order to enter an attractive market. As a result, they get careless in their selection process and mistakenly trade poor partner quality for quick action. Partners are often selected only for short-term or political reasons. When the situation changes and the partner has nothing more to offer, the relationship often ends. Let me give you an example.

One large North American multinational enterprise (MNE) which had for years operated a wholly owned subsidiary in a developing country found itself constrained by local government regulations on foreign ownership which limited the repatriation of dividends. To expand the business and to remit dividends, a significant level of local equity participation was encouraged. A joint venture was the obvious solution and a minority joint venture would permit the maximum local investment base and repatriation of the maximum allowable dividends. This was a significant change for the company, which had operated primarily through wholly owned subsidiaries or joint ventures that it controlled.

The company searched for a local corporation or individual who would not be actively involved in the business. The legal requirements regarding ownership would be met and the North American parent could control and run the joint venture. An apparently satisfactory partner was found, and more than a year was spent completing the financial and legal arrangements. Within six months of starting the joint venture, however, there was substantial conflict between the partners over differences of opinion about strategy and operating procedures. The relationship deteriorated during the next three years over a variety of issues and ended in the local courts. The issue brought to the court was the inappropriate procedures used by the local partner in distributing stock to the local employees as part of the "nationalization" process. The general consensus at the North American parent was that the short-term financial gain probably did not offset the significant costs incurred in management time, direct expenses, stress on employees, and possible damage to the firm's reputation in that part of the world. This company was not committed to the use of the minority joint venture form and did not have a long-term need for its partner. It essentially wanted to buy his nationality. The marriage of convenience did not work.

Okay, so it looks like taking a short cut is a bad idea. What does the best partnership look like?

To be successful, a partnership must operate on the principle of fair exchange. There must be value in the relationship for both parties. Major differences in the performance of joint ventures relate to whether there exists a long-term need and commitment between the partners. "Need" refers to the requirement for skills or resources in the venture such as access to raw materials, distribution channels, labor, political connections, and local knowledge. Unfortunately, there is a tendency to think of these needs primarily from the perspective of the foreign parent.

In my opinion, the best joint venturers—meaning those who work toward ensuring the long-term viability of the business—are the companies that recognize their specific long-term needs and recruit partners to fill these needs. They also recognize the needs of their local partner and how they will fill those needs.

Who is likely to be better at finding good local managers?

Local partners are sometimes more likely to have access to competent local managers than do foreign firms. In all countries the demand for qualified managers by foreign firms and by local firms is high. In some countries this pressure is increased by incentive systems encouraging the "localization" or "indigenization" of human resources in foreign companies and joint ventures. However, even in those countries where an adequate supply of trained managers exists, these good local managers are sometimes not as accessible to foreign firms.

Why not?

Some local managers avoid foreign firms in favor of working for local firms, or starting their own businesses. Some had been denied promotions that went to expatriates from the foreign company or foreign parent. They believed that it was almost impossible to advance to senior executive positions in foreign firms or foreign controlled joint ventures. The foreign parent, therefore, needs to consider carefully how it will assign expatriates to the venture so that it can develop its executives without interfering with the development and progression of the local managers. Once this potential conflict has been identified, the partners together can work out a plan to satisfy the needs of both.

Local partners also have needs to which the foreign parent can contribute. Technology can be an important contribution—if the foreign parent is undertaking regular technological improvements. Many joint ventures in emerging markets have collapsed after the simple technology provided by the foreign parent had been assimilated by the local partner and there was no upgrading of it. The local partner may feel there is no longer a major advantage to having a foreign partner, and strike out alone. For its part, the foreign parent may feel betrayed since it provided the technology with a view towards developing a long-term relationship and no longer receives the expected stream of earnings.

There may also be a need for export opportunities. Given a local partner's interest in increasing total sales and generating foreign exchange, some foreign parents have ensured that they will be needed over the long-term by providing, incrementally, access to their distribution network, usually on a regional basis.

Better performing companies use the joint venture structure voluntarily. Foreign parent companies choose local partners for their knowledge of the local economy, politics and customs and to provide managers. These foreign partners view these needs as continuing and long-term.

A lot of Western corporations tend to think that local knowledge is a short-term need and that the company will learn quickly all they need about that market. However, the local scene keeps changing. New players appear, as well as new attitudes, regulations and laws. Learning must keep pace.

Won't expatriates do the trick?

Sometimes, but even expatriates living in the country can be out of touch with the country and culture. They may become insulated from reality by the exclusiveness of the expatriate community and by acceptance of this community's sometimes-inaccurate perceptions of local people and conditions. Local people can fill this need best. As one international V.P. noted, "In many developing countries, it takes about twenty years to completely understand the local system—and we just can't leave our expatriate managers there that long."

Does it make sense to use the government as a partner?

The temptation to have a local politician or government official as a joint venture partner is often strong. However, governments change. A partner should be expected to bring more to the partnership than political position or contacts. A partner should be able to make a contribution to the on-going operation. The best advice seems to be: use industrialists of some stature in the same or a similar business—if you can find them. The next best choice would be a firm that offers a complementary service such as product distribution. As you move further from your business base, the ability of your partner to contribute substantially to the venture and to provide qualified general managers declines.

How long does it take to find a partner?

Finding the right partner takes time and effort, and there is no substitute for active, rigorous exploration. I am always amazed at how some partners were found. Some had been met "fortuitously" at cocktail parties, or in a hotel bar. Non-rigorous search for a partner may result in taking the first person who comes along, which most likely is a mistake. Twelve to eighteen months is not an unusual amount of time spent in finding and selecting a partner.

One reason finding a partner can take so long is that quality business people in many developing countries are likely to be more relationship-oriented than North Americans. They want to establish a personal relationship first and then do business. Initially, they want to focus on the North American as a person. Do they feel comfortable with and trust him? However, North Americans usually want to discuss business right away. In North America, we generally conduct business, and out of the business a personal relationship might develop. Building relationships takes time and patience, commodities we often lack.

Are there any other things one needs to consider in regards to whether the partner possesses the necessary skills?

A few things, yes. First, it is important to distinguish between the skills a partner possesses and what the JV needs to succeed. These may not be the same thing. Second, you'll want to make sure that your proposed partner firm has been reinvesting and upgrading its skills, and not just coasting along.

How do you do that?

You measure it. If you are attracted to a partner because of their technical skills, you get details on whether their technical staff has grown or shrunk in recent years, whether they have lost or added any key people, things like that. Ask lots of questions and request lots of evidence that the skill or resource you think you are buying does in fact exist.

Now what about getting access to these skills? Some of the potential partners we considered seemed to be involved in a lot of businesses. One of our concerns was that some had so many other commitments then we'd never get much access. Do you ever see this?

Foreign parents often have to face the issue of multiple business interests on the part of their local partners. They should not be unrealistically scared away from an excellent local partner because of the partner's seemingly unfocused diversity of interests. However, it is a legitimate concern that such interests will dilute the partner's attention to the joint venture unless a solid local management team is put into place. This is an area in which expectations must be established clearly. For its part, the foreign parent has a responsibility to provide quality expatriates who can contribute to the venture and not use it as a dumping ground for soon-to-be-retiring executives or merely as a training ground for inexperienced people.

Anything else?

You'll also want to be sure that you are able to use the skills/resources being made available to you. You need to think about ease of access.

I'm not sure I understand what you mean. Do you have an example?

Let me give you three examples. First, you may have a local partner who is going to provide a number of strong local managers. You'll probably then want to make sure that the people you send to the joint venture can communicate in the local language. Many years ago, I vividly remember sitting with senior executives from one of the major automakers in Detroit. They were looking for advice on entering China via joint venture. We asked them a few "innocent" questions about their preparedness. Of particular interest to us was their ability to access the resources and knowledge any partner might make available. So we asked, "How many of your top 1,000 executives/managers speak Chinese?" Long pause, no answer. "How many of your top 1,000 executives/managers are of Chinese descent?" Long pause, and finally a terse answer: "We don't know. We've obviously got some homework to do."

A second similar example would be if you were providing technology to a joint venture. Here you need to verify that the relevant people in the JV are technically literate. Otherwise, a lot of useful interactions won't be possible.

A third example is from Cummins. They have a large business in emerging markets and use lots of joint ventures. One of the things they emphasize is the need to synchronize information flows between the JV and themselves. As with the two previous examples, it comes down in part to being truly able to understand, and access, what is going on in the JV.

8

Compatibility

The third consideration in the partner selection process relates to compatibility. Essentially it asks how well the partners will get along with each other.

Okay, but Peter isn't this a nice-to-have issue, rather than a have-to-have issue? I mean there is inevitably lots of people we all work with on a day-to-day basis that we aren't best pals with. But we usually find a way to get along.

Of course you do. You're a professional. That said however, for a variety of reasons which I'll explain, I'll still argue that compatibility matters.

Yeah, but I'm not looking for a spouse. I'm looking for a business partner, someone to make money with. To me, it ought to be far more important that any partner is competent.

Okay, but why choose one over the other?

What do you mean?

Have a look at this simple 2 × 2 matrix.

Partner selection: Comfort versus competence.

	Lower competence	Higher competence
Higher comfort	Unstable	Target
Lower comfort	Non-starter	Unstable

In my experience, too many joint ventures are established where one finds a competent partner, but it is not someone with whom you particularly like to spend a lot of time.

But what's so wrong with that?

If there is someone with whom you don't want to spend much time, you'll find ways not to spend time with them. It's just human nature. This is a problem with joint ventures, because at various stages in their development, there is a need for the partners to work closely together if they are to achieve their potential.

Okay, I'll concede that maybe I should be more than neutral about the value of compatibility. But isn't it possible to place too much emphasis on compatibility?

If it comes at the expense of competence, absolutely yes. You want both comfort and competence.

But isn't it tough to find partners who can meet both criteria?

It certainly takes some work. But the fact that there are tens of thousands of equity joint ventures around the world that have been in business for a decade or more, certainly suggests that it is possible.

How do you know if you are compatible, or going to be compatible?

There are a few ways.

Potential partners can be visited in their milieu to see how they live and how they run their business. This will give you a feel for their operating style.

It is also useful to find ways in which to work together on smaller projects to "test" the working relationship. It is easier and more satisfactory to increase investment in a small project than to write-off one's large investment.

Are there other reasons you feel compatibility matters?

Yes. Two others. The next relates to the whole issue of organizational climate similarity, while the last relates to a story I'll share about one of the joint venture facilitations.

What do you mean by organizational climate similarity?

Organizational climate is the observable practices of an organization. My basic argument is that joint ventures between partners having more dissimilar organizational climates incur different and higher organizational costs, which in turn negatively effect overall firm performance.

What would these organizational costs look like?

Depending on the degree of organizational climate dissimilarity present in a joint venture, several items cause joint ventures to experience different levels of organizational costs: avoiding coordination and control losses, decreasing uncertainty, and decreasing the risk of opportunistic behavior.

What do you mean by avoiding coordination and control losses?

When firms work together, it is desirable that they have similar organizational climates, since this homogeneity avoids losses in co-ordination and control that are normally associated with diversity. Differences in organizational climates of firms trying to work together lead to differences in management practices and values. These differences may, in turn, lead to cultural ambiguity and losses when people from different organizational climates work together. In turn, these losses increase the cost of conducting the business.

Coordination and control losses may result from a variety of different situations; for example, from one parent firm not being able to understand what another parent firm does, because of ineffective communication between the two firms (organizational communication flow is a dimension of organizational climate). This ineffective communication may result from the parent firms' organizational climates being so different that it is hard for the firms to know how to relate to each other. For example, firm A may be very hierarchical, with upper management approving most decisions, while firm B may have few levels of hierarchy and workers who are empowered to make decisions. A worker in firm B might try to ask a worker in firm A about his opinion on a certain issue. However, the worker in firm A may be reluctant to give his opinion, without first consulting his manager. The worker in firm B may misinterpret this reluctance as an attempt not to co-operate. This misinterpretation may, in turn, lead to retaliation of workers in firm B, or at least frustration at the firm A worker's unwillingness to co-operate. Clearly, the troubles caused by the two firms' differing communication patterns will increase the organizational costs of using the joint venture described above, compared to a joint venture where both parents have similar communication flow patterns. Such losses may also result, because one firm's organizational climate is more oriented towards taking risks, than is the other firms'. Thus, it is desirable that parties involved in a joint venture have similar organizational climates, so that they can avoid such losses and minimize organizational costs.

How do you minimize uncertainty?

It is often difficult to know how to value or measure the worth of a firm's contribution to a joint venture. For example, a local firm may promise to provide its potential foreign partner with many customers and with contacts to help them navigate through the bureaucracy. It is hard to know in advance how valuable these customers will be, or how much help the contacts will provide. When such measurement difficulties exist, it is often desirable when forming a joint venture to reduce uncertainty and minimize the problems of one of the partners not delivering on its commitment and essentially getting a free ride.

When two parties in a joint venture have similar organizational climates, they are more likely to have similar measurement and control systems. Certain transactions possess uncertainties, information asymmetries, and free rider problems that are especially well suited to certain measurement and control systems (organizational climates). Thus, two parent firms having similar organizational climates are likely to experience similar efficiency improvements.

Uncertainty causes parent firms to make more complicated JV contracts, spend more time monitoring the environment and the other parties involved in the joint venture, and spend more time and resources preparing for different contingences. Clearly, all of these activities cost something, and thus the presence of uncertainty increases the organizational costs. Therefore, the greater the uncertainty, the poorer the joint venture is likely to perform, because organizational costs will increase due to greater uncertainty, because increased monitoring will be necessary. Thus, for a joint venture to perform better, it is desirable for uncertainty to be decreased.

Your third point was about decreasing opportunism. What is this?

The threat of opportunistic behavior initially drives many partners to form a JV. The JV organizational structure reduces the costs of opportunism at the expense of increasing bureaucratic or administrative costs. If properly developed, trust can reduce the threat of opportunism and make the JV mode the most efficient one in some cases.

Differences in organizational climates may also result in one partner misinterpreting, as opportunistic, the actions of the other partner. When one partner stops exercising restraint, the other partner's incentive to continue to exercise restraint decreases significantly. As a result, this misunderstanding, based on differences of organizational climate, may lead to a real attempt to engage in opportunistic actions, often irreversibly ending restraint and impairing joint venture performance.

Therefore, forming a joint venture with a firm that has a more similar organizational climate, and thus is more predisposed to avoid opportunistic behavior, is desirable. By being less predisposed towards opportunistic behavior, the joint venture can avoid expensive safeguards against such behavior (e.g., frequent meetings, visit to the JV by each parent, daily reports, or email messages, constraints on managerial action). The lower costs associated with reducing the threat of opportunism will translate into higher performance, both in terms of satisfaction and in terms of financial outcomes.

In summary, to have the best chance of achieving optimal JV performance, it is important for firms considering a joint venture to select a partner that has an organizational climate similar to their own. It is desirable to create an organizational climate at the JV level that is similar to the foreign parent's organizational climate. This is the most important organizational climate dissimilarity relationship on which to focus. Further, dissimilarity in organizational climate between parent firms is arguably more important in determining IJV success than dissimilarity in national culture.

Okay. I think I understand what you are saying. Now, what about that story.

Right. Some years ago, I did a joint venture facilitation between a small family-owned company that was proposing to set up a joint venture with a division of a Fortune 100 company. The president of the small company and the divisional president of the large company had been able to quite rightly establish that a strong strategic logic existed for them to be considering such a step. They'd met numerous times over the previous six months, and had developed a strong personal relationship. They then decided to more actively involve their respective senior management teams, in the discussions, and invited me in to facilitate a meeting.

The bigger company, let's call it Richco, was a highly profitable firm, with lots of resources behind it. The smaller company was in an industry where it was hard to generate big profits as a smaller player. As a result, it was not as resource rich as Richco.

I was asked where we should meet and as per my usual policy, suggested we should meet at a neutral site. The Richco president responded by saying that his parent company maintained several corporate retreat/training centers, and that one of them was available at no charge for the period we were targeting. He added that one of Richco's corporate jets was also available at that time to pick up and return everyone, again at no charge. The president of the small company thought this sounded great, and readily agreed, despite my recommendation otherwise. I said that I would take a commercial flight.

Peter: let me say this with the greatest respect, but "Are you nuts?" A corporate jet? Think about the convenience! The bragging rights!

Trust me, I did think about all that, but still concluded it was going to send the wrong messages. Anyways, we all eventually arrived at their retreat. A butler took our coats, someone delivered our luggage to our respective suites, and we were individually introduced to the head chef who asked us what we might wish to have that evening. Anyways you get the picture. The place was palatial. There were about 15 full time staff available for the nine of us: the two presidents, three senior executives from each company, and me. We had agreed in advance that we would spend the evening getting to know each other and relaxing, and get down to work at 8:00 a.m. the next morning. Since the senior management teams didn't know each other all that well, this seemed sensible to me. They had a large, very well-stocked bar where everyone met both before and after dinner.

Over the next seven hours, from about 4:00 in the afternoon until about 11:00 p.m., I watched a very interesting phenomena unfold. First off, it was clear to everyone that the two presidents very much liked the idea of the joint venture, and had built a good rapport with each other. When everyone moved to the bar area again after dinner, they sat at one end of it, somewhat off by themselves. To put the most positive spin on things, I think their intent in doing so was to allow the respective management teams the space to get to know each other. This didn't exactly happen. By about 10:00 p.m., the three senior guys from Richco were talking only to each other, as were the three senior folks from the smaller firm. I made a couple of attempts to get all six together at one table, but this attempt was deftly rebuffed by one of the Richco guys.

In the best tradition of relationship building, I nonetheless decided to sacrifice my liver, and moved back and forth between the groups, having a drink with each. Most of the time, I simply smiled and listened.

At each table, I began to hear a different variation on the same disquieting tune. The common theme was "Why are we talking to these guys?"

The executives from Richco were commenting on the fact that their counterparts didn't seem very sophisticated, either in their business practices, dress, vocabulary, or manner. One went so far as to say "I guess we're going to have to put up with these guys for six months or so because the Prez really wants this deal to happen. Meanwhile, the senior people from the smaller company seemed to have similarly developed distaste for their counterparts. The gist of their comments was along the lines of "These guys have never actually managed anything. They have big staffs, and are so far removed from an operating level, I don't know if we could trust them with the keys to the washroom."

Wow. So what did you do?

I went to bed.

You went to bed? With a problem like that staring you in the face? How could you?

Ah. I neglected to mention that by this time, the two presidents had each consumed what appeared to me to be rather large quantities of alcohol. I knew I needed to urgently speak with them, but needed to do so when they were stone sober. So I said nothing that evening, other than requesting that the three of us meet at 7:45 a.m. They agreed.

We met the next morning sharply at 7:45 and I quickly explained, without naming names, some of the comments I'd heard the previous evening, and my own conclusion that their respective management teams were far from being on-board with respect to the proposed joint venture. Both looked at me with disbelief, both saying that they thought I'd misread the situation. I acknowledged that this was possible but urged them to meet with their respective senior management teams before the nine of us convened at 8:00 a.m. I did not join either meeting.

8:00 a.m. came and went and the only people in the dining room were three waiters and me. 8:15—same situation. 8:30—same situation. At about 8:40, both presidents joined me in the dining room and confirmed that I had not misread the situation. Both were somewhat angry—I'm not sure with themselves or their senior managers. We agreed that I should still proceed with my presentation material—since everyone was present—and they "obviously have got something to learn about joint ventures." They further agreed, under the circumstances, we probably would not require 1½ full days, as originally planned. We had a pleasant enough, although sometimes stiff, meeting until mid-afternoon, and everyone went home.

You must have been very upset.

No, to the contrary. This was a joint venture that shouldn't have happened, and didn't. To me this was a very successful outcome. Both companies saved themselves a lot of legal and administrative expenses. The reason I share the story is that I think it illustrates a final point about partner compatibility, that is, that it has to exist at multiple levels in the organization.

PART 4

Shape and Design

9

What Is the Investment Necessary for Success?

Okay David, we've now covered the basics of strategic logic, and partnership and fit. Ready to move on to the next section—shape and design?

Absolutely.

There are three areas we need to cover with respect to shape and design. These respectively relate to the investment necessary for success, control, and negotiations. Let's consider them in turn.

Great.

Every joint venture requires a legal document that lays out the key elements of the actual agreement. These documents vary greatly in their length and complexity.

Is there an ideal length?

I don't know if anyone would ever agree on an answer to that question! Your legal department or outside counsel will want to be as thorough as possible. The reality of course is that one can never cover off all the issues that might arise in any joint venture. Any contract that tries to do so lands up being incredibly long, sometimes hundreds of pages. This contract forms the basis for discussions with the potential partner that can then lead to many months and sometimes over a year of discussions.

Sounds pretty unwieldy.

It can be.

So what do you do?

Start with what is crucial to you, and to the future success of the JV. Make sure that this is covered in the agreement. If there are some assumptions that are particularly important to you, clarify them. Here's a graphic that starts to speak to this point.

Scope of activity

Narrow	vs.	Wide
Single, geographic market	vs.	Multi-country
Single function	vs.	Complete value chain
Single industry/customer group	vs.	Multi-industry
Modest investment	vs.	Large scale
Existing business	vs.	New business
Limited term	vs.	Forever

This seems pretty straightforward.

It is straightforward, as long as you remember to actually deal with these points. That way, there is less confusion both now and later.

Fair enough. Now all of these points on the graphic deal with a joint venture's scope of activity. What else has to be in the agreement?

All the usual things: clarification of who is going to manage what; the composition and role of the board; how disagreements or deadlocks will be handled; any representations or warranties; organization structure; capitalization; contracts between the partners; rights and obligations regarding intellectual property; termination; etc…

Termination? Is it a good idea to talk about possible break up even before you've gotten started?

On balance, yes. Sometimes despite best efforts, there are irreconcilable differences. So it's better to discuss how you'd both deal with this issue in the hopefully unlikely event it happens, and to discuss it when it isn't a problem.

How might this work?

One of the most common approaches is what's colloquially known as a shotgun clause. This allows either partner to name a price it is willing to pay to buy out the other's shares. Once such a step is taken however, the other partner can either sell out at that price per share, or buy its partner's shares at the same price. This ensures any offers made are fairer, closer to a market value.

So, if I can summarize, you want to emphasize the quality of the relationship as much as you can, but that said, not to neglect the legal agreement.

That's it.

Now before we get into issues around both control and negotiations, I want to jump ahead for a moment. It links to the distinction you've just made between the soft side—things such as relationships, and the hard side—things such as contracts. What I'm getting at is that both are important, not one at the expense of the other. Further, both will continue to be important even after you've done the deal.

Can you go into a little more detail about what you mean?

Sure. Joint ventures need close and continuing attention, particularly in their early months. In addition to establishing a healthy working relationship between the parents and the venture general manager, managers should be on the lookout for the impact that cultural differences may be having on the venture and for the emergence of unforeseen inequities.

International joint ventures, like any type of international activity, require managers of different national cultures to work together. This requires the selection of capable people in key roles. Unless managers have been sensitized to the characteristics of the culture that they are dealing with, this can lead to misunderstandings and serious problems. For example, many Western managers are frustrated by the slow, consensus-oriented decision-making style of the Japanese. Equally, the Japanese find American individualistic decision making to be surprising, as the decisions are made so quickly, but the implementation is often so slow. Firms that are sophisticated in the use of international joint ventures are well aware of such problems and have taken action to minimize them through such things as cultural sensitivity training for their managers.

It is important to remember that cultural differences do not just arise from differences in nationality. For example:

- Small firms working with large partners are often surprised and dismayed by the fact that it can take months, rather than days, to

get approval of a new project. In some cases the cultural differences appear to be greater between small and large firms of the same nationality than, say, between multinationals of different nationality, particularly if the multinationals are in the same industry.
- Firms working with two partners from the same country have been surprised to find how different the companies are in cultural habits. A firm headquartered in a rural area may be a very different company from one run from a major metropolitan center.
- Cultural differences between managers working in different functional areas may be greater than those between managers in the same function in different firms. European engineers, for example, discovered when discussing a potential joint venture with an American partner that they had more in common with the American engineers than with the marketing people in their own company.

Anything else besides cultural difference?

A very common joint venture problem is that the objectives of the parents, which coincided when the venture was formed, diverge over time. Unintended inequities may arise during the life of a venture. Due to an unforeseen circumstance, one parent may be winning from the venture while the other is losing.

Can you provide an example of an "unforeseen circumstance"?

Sure. The easiest example would be a rapidly fluctuating change in the exchange rate in one of the two partners' countries. If the value of my home country currency goes up, it makes it harder to profitably export because most of my costs are denominated in the home currency. As your joint venture partner, if I'm dependent on exports, I've now got a big problem.

So what should happen?

In such a situation, a change in the original agreement should be considered, so the hardship is shared between the parents.

Any checklist of the things to be considered when forming a joint venture can be very lengthy. It is important to recognize that such a list will vary somewhat depending on where the international joint venture is established. For example, the characteristics of joint ventures will vary according to whether they are established in developed versus developing countries.

So if I have this right, you're saying beyond the physical investment that is going to be necessary for JV success, there is also an attitudinal investment that is necessary, a commitment. The JV will require continuing top management attention, not just attention at startup. Everyone ought to watch for inequities, and maintain a degree of flexibility.

Exactly so.

10

Control and Influence

Which *partner should make the day-to-day decisions in a joint venture? My partner and I have been having quite a discussion about control.*

The division of management control between joint venture partners has been a long-standing matter of contention. Some MNEs want dominant control of the JV's management. Others argue that both MNE and local partners should share management if the JV is to be successful. As we've discussed, the most common JV structure, at least in emerging markets, is the one in which an MNE contributes technology and a local partner contributes local knowledge-related skills. In such JVs, performance is arguably driven by the resource complementarity between the partners. Low performance is thus a consequence of a lack of, or erosion of, resource complementarity between the partners. However, the complementary resources brought by the partners to the venture represent only "potential" complementarity. To actually realize the resource complementarity available between the partners, firms have to deal with the partition of management control between them.

Before we go on, what do you mean by control? I want to be sure we are both working from a common understanding.

Control is the influence exercised by the parents over the management of the venture. The control that is partitioned between the parents represents the relative influence of each parent on the management of the JV. Control is a conduit through which parents' specific advantages or capabilities are transferred to the venture. If control is not properly partitioned between the partners, then performance is likely to suffer because of ineffective transfer of the parents' specific advantages to the JV. By proper partitioning of the JV's management control, I mean a fit between the parent's specific advantages transferred to the venture and the parent's control over the corresponding value-creation activities of JV management.

How many control options are available?

Four broad control options are available:

1. Each JV partner controls its own specific advantages (split control management).
2. Both partners share control over all advantages (shared management or shared control).
3. The MNE partner assumes a dominant control over all firm advantages (MNE partner-dominant management).
4. The local emerging-market partner assumes a dominant control over all firm advantages (local partner-dominant management).

Figure 10.1 provides a framework to analyze these four options. This framework takes the MNE partner's perspective. The vertical axis represents the extent to which an MNE partner exercises control over its

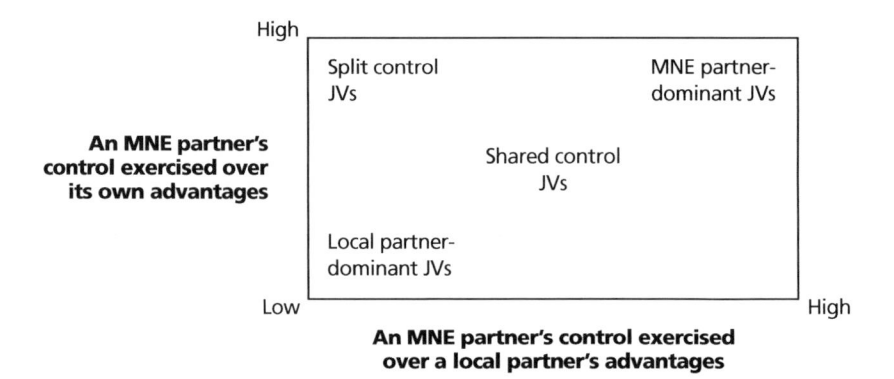

Figure 10.1 Four ways of partitioning control between JV partners.

own advantages, and the horizontal axis represents the extent to which an MNE partner exercises control over a local partner's advantages. The combination of these two dimensions generates the four types of international JV corresponding to the four options available to MNE and local emerging market partners: one high in both dimensions (or what we call MNE partner-dominant JVs), another low in both dimensions (what we call local-partner-dominant JVs), a third high in the dimension of MNE partners' control exercised over their own advantages but low in the dimension of MNE partners' control exercised over local partners' advantages (what we call split control JVs), and the fourth medium in both dimensions (what we call shared management or shared control JVs).

Can you provide the basic argument and an example of each view?

Sure. The argument for one partner-dominant ventures is that they are easier to manage, and hence produce better performance. Certainly everyone would agree that the shared nature of JV management could make JVs difficult to manage. As we've discussed, a variety of behavioral, cultural, and managerial differences between parent firms makes effective management of a JV a demanding task in terms of time and effort. Some have argued that the management difficulty is amplified in shared management ventures more than in one-partner-dominant ventures, given that the former involve greater interaction between parent firms.

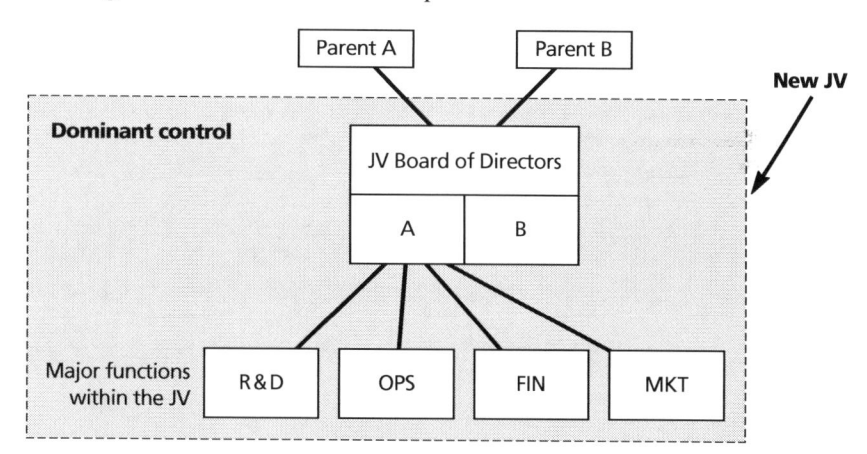

An example of a JV where one partner exercised dominant control was Toppan Moore. In this multi-billion dollar JV, the local partner, Toppan Printing of Japan, had dominant control while the North American partner, Moore Business Forms of Toronto, took a lesser role. Moore accepted not having a bigger role in the JV because they didn't know a lot about the Japanese market in the beginning. In the early stages, Moore provided

72 ▪ *Joint Venturing*

cutting-edge proprietary technology, equipment, and production-management systems to their partner. Twenty-five years after the establishment of this JV, the new president of Toppan Moore commented on the reasons for its success:

> Moore provided good circumstances for the development of the company. Moore is a very caring parent. They made a sincere effort to launch the company. They gave us a lot of autonomy. They didn't interfere. We were able to adopt certain managerial methods and arrange them to fit with Japanese business customs. Moore has a long-term view. We make decisions on personnel, investment and fund raising without detailed consultation. We were able to manage freely, and we have adopted many Japanese principles such as a long-term focus, interdependence among companies, and a management style based on loyalty and human feeling. Toppan Moore is very much a traditional Japanese company.

What about shared management ventures?

The argument for shared management ventures is that sharing control with a local partner is a vehicle for tapping country-specific advantages embedded within a local partner. Therefore, the more control an MNE parent shares with a local partner, the more country-specific advantages the MNE parent will acquire to augment its firm-specific advantages. Because sharing control will augment the firm-specific advantages of both the MNE and the local partner more than dominant control does, shared management ventures should exhibit superior performance.

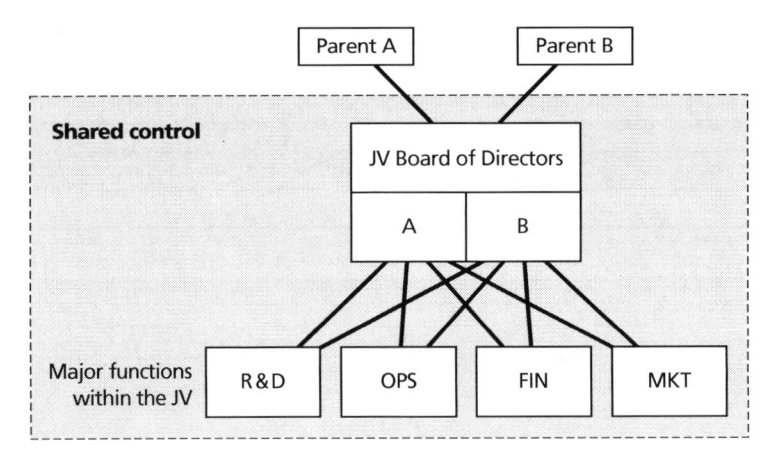

I don't like all those lines between the various functional areas, and the JV Board. It sort of reminds me of a matrix-style structure, which I can tell you first hand is pretty unwieldy.

Your reaction is not unlike that of Bundy Asia Pacific in regards to one of their early JVs in China. Internally, the nature of the 50:50 share holding and the need for consensus on all major decisions had made their JV difficult to manage efficiently. The difficulty mainly came from the partners' differences in objectives and systems. The difference in objectives between partners in China had been described as "in the same bed but different dreams." What the local government partner wanted from the JV were local economic development, advanced technology transfer, capital infusion and local employment. The second Chinese partner was more interested in learning advanced technology and management skills, as well as generating some rapid returns. Bundy, like most foreign investors, wished for market share and profitability. Moreover, although Chinese law allowed a joint venture to set up its system to fit its own needs and desires, neither of the two Chinese partners nor the Chinese employees could quickly adapt to a Western management system. The Chinese partners wanted to appreciate and learn the way in which Bundy ran the business, but they found it difficult to break with their long-existing framework, particularly in a short period of time. Under these circumstances, the equally shared joint venture resulted in endless conflicts.

What's the next option?

In split control ventures, the activities of control chosen by the parents are matched with their respective firm-specific advantages. Essentially you control or manage those activities you are contributing to the JV. These are assumed to be those that you are able to better manage than your partner.

An example of a split control JV would be Sun Life Financial's venture with China Everbright Group. Sun Life Financial's strategy was to partner in China with a respected and prestigious firm that had clout with the national and local authorities. Sun Life wanted to create an entity that was "Chinese in operation in spirit with Western business practices, management and technology." China Everbright Group was a large, state-owned entity. In this JV, each side owned 50% of the equity, and split the decision-making duties, with four board members being appointed from each partner. In the start up period, Sun Life was responsible for the day-to-day operations while Everbright shared its distribution network and management's local expertise and ability to deal with the governments in seeking approvals.

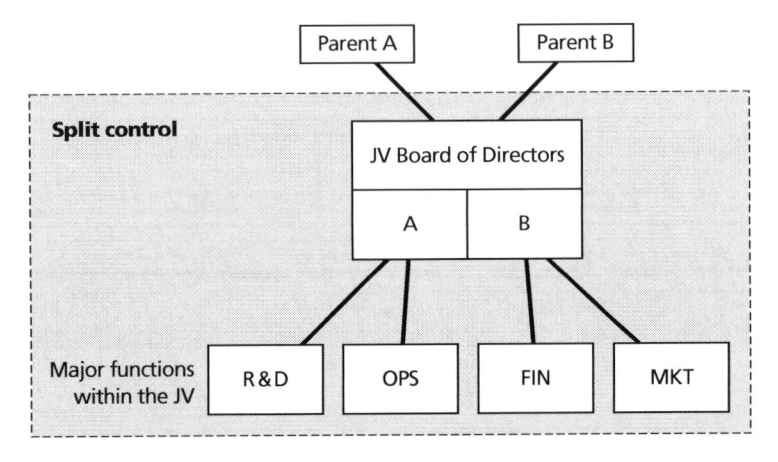

```
                    ┌──────────┐     ┌──────────┐
                    │ Parent A │     │ Parent B │
                    └────┬─────┘     └────┬─────┘
┌────────────────────────┼────────────────┼──────────────────────┐
│ Split control          │                │                      │
│                    ┌───┴────────────────┴───┐                  │
│                    │  JV Board of Directors │                  │
│                    ├────────────┬───────────┤                  │
│                    │     A      │     B     │                  │
│                    └────────────┴───────────┘                  │
│                                                                │
│ Major functions  ┌─────┐   ┌─────┐   ┌─────┐   ┌─────┐        │
│ within the JV    │ R&D │   │ OPS │   │ FIN │   │ MKT │        │
│                  └─────┘   └─────┘   └─────┘   └─────┘        │
└────────────────────────────────────────────────────────────────┘
```

So which one is best?

On balance, JVs following split control management perform better than any other approach. No performance differences exist among the remaining three types of management, at least in emerging markets. This suggests that MNEs and local partners should split control: that is, choose the activities to control so that those chosen activities can be matched with their respective complementary resources. In other words, the partner who has the skills or the resources needed to perform particular value-creation activities of the JV should control those activities in the JV.

It's hard to argue against the logic of matching or fitting one's contributions to those areas you control. It seems to me that the choices other than split control will all have limitations.

Agreed. The fit between each parent's firm-specific advantages and parent's control over the corresponding activities of JV management is less emphasized in shared control ventures. In shared control JVs with both partners exercising influence over all major decisions, a misalignment, rather than fit, between the parents' firm-specific advantages and the activities of control chosen by the parents is likely to prevail. The prevalence of the misalignment, in turn, contributes to low JV performance, versus in split control ventures. This negative effect of the misalignment on JV performance also explains the lower performance found in MNE or local-partner-dominant ventures. As one of the partners exercises dominant control over the JV's management, single-partner-dominant ventures experience the misalignment as much as shared control ventures.

Now that I think more about it, it really doesn't make sense to have a "joint" venture, if you actually want to control everything. So when we use joint ventures, it does seem obvious that we should split control of the various functions with our partner.

Right. Now so far we've been discussing a macro perspective on control. There are also more specific mechanisms available that will allow either partner to exact control or influence in the JV.

There is more than one?

There are actually quite a few, and many of them are of course the same sorts of things you'd see in any business.

Can we talk about some of the different types?

Sure. Let's start with the JV's board of directors. In my experience, JV boards vary enormously. Some include people who have previous experience with joint ventures, while others are composed of people who are learning on the job about JVs. Clearly the former is preferable. Some have people with excellent skills in diplomacy and persuasion while unfortunate others include people with a my-way-or-the-highway attitude. Some boards rely on their equity ownership level as the basis for control or influence, while in others there is a recognition that one doesn't have to have a huge equity position in order to exercise a lot of sway.

Can you have meaningful influence as a minority equity partner?

Absolutely. For example, at the Board level in some JVs, both partners may have veto right on expenditures over a certain dollar amount. This means that minority partners can have just as much voice as the majority partner.

What would be a second type of mechanism for influence/control?

Staffing. You can provide some of your people to the JV. The key positions of course are the general manager's role, and some of the top functional manager positions.

Is there an ideal number of expatriates that one might send to any JV in these roles?

I don't think anyone would agree on an answer to that question. We do know that firms use expatriates for three main reasons: (1) control, (2) to develop or train their own people, and (3) to transfer skills or technology to the joint venture or subsidiary. And not surprisingly, one's partner will have quite different reactions to expatriates, depending on the reason they've been sent to the JV.

How so?

Let's consider each of the three reasons in turn. (1) Expatriates who are sent in order to control that function, which their parent company is contributing, are typically accepted, given their competency. (2) People who are sent by a parent company to help them gain international experience, are sometimes resented at the local level unless they are seen as adding a lot of value, and/or if the parent company is paying some or all of their salary rather than charging it against the JV. (3) People who are sent to a JV for technology transfer purposes are typically welcomed, particularly if they don't stay terribly long and if they don't come with a big cost being charged against the JV.

One really has to think about how each major staffing decision will be interpreted by their partner, don't they?

Yes.

Now let me comment briefly on a third possible mechanism for control/influence. One can use all of the usual corporate management systems and processes. Here I'm referring to everything from planning, capital budgeting, performance measurement systems, compensation packages, promotions, and various other policies and procedures. Any of these can be customized at the JV level for the purposes of control/influence.

Any other mechanisms?

Two more. The first of these is the provision of parent company services. Some parent companies make available to their joint ventures a variety of their resources, at little or no cost. For example, a parent firm may be doing a customized training program on some subject. Since the variable costs of adding one more person to a training program tend to be pretty low, they can gain a lot of mileage by offering a spot on the program to someone from the JV. The person from the JV gets to know a bunch of people from that parent, which in turn can subtly lead to that parent having more influence.

Makes sense. What's the last one?

Informal mechanisms. Here I'm specifically referring to the role of personal visits, and phone calls. Let me share a view on both. Over the years, I've come across a few companies who insist that the executives who go to visit their joint ventures should not immediately return home after their formal meeting agenda items have been dealt with. They want their executives to spend social time with their local joint venture partners. In fact some have gone so far as to urge their executives who have, say, two days of meetings, to spend an extra day with the partners, either golfing, or visiting museums, whatever.

This would be heresy in my company. Social time is nice, but these have got to be busy guys. This sounds to me like it could be a waste of potentially productive hours. Why would they do this?

Because they place a lot of value on the relationship. What they are trying to work toward is the development of trust between the partners. They want trust because they feel—rightfully in my view—that trust is the most efficient thing that one can have in business. They would argue that if the partners trust each other, little issues would be much less likely to turn into big issues, because they'll be able to resolve most differences in a spirit of goodwill.

Okay, that makes sense. But how do you get to trust?

Well it obviously won't happen by leaving your wallet on the table and seeing if your partner swipes your cash. You can't ever guarantee that real trust will develop. All you can do is create some conditions where it has the chance to develop. And the prime condition to achieve this potential is to spend time together.

I can see the logic of this, although it sure would represent a change in our corporate culture.

Would that be a bad thing?

I'm starting to think maybe not.

The last point I was going to mention was in regards to phone calls. I've seen some JV board members who have the habit of calling their partner every month. They don't wait for semi-annual Board meetings. They stay in very regular touch. This gives them a sort of early warning if problems are developing, and helps to maintain the relationship.

11

Negotiating the Joint Venture

One *of my biggest concerns is how to approach the whole issue of negotiating a joint venture. Can we talk about this one Peter?*

Sure. Let's do it with an example that is typical of many joint ventures. In this example, a Malaysian company, Nora Holdings Sdn Bhd (Nora), was in the process of trying to establish a joint venture in Malaysia with a Finnish company, Sakari Oy (Sakari). The rationale for the formation of the joint venture was for Nora to acquire knowledge of Sakari's telecommunications switching technology and for Sakari to gain access to the Malaysian market and ultimately knowledge of south East Asia opportunities. To achieve these objectives, the joint-venture company would produce digital switching exchanges based on Sakari's system to initially fulfill a five-year contract from Malaysia's national telecom company, TMB.

The formation of a joint venture seemed feasible since it would serve the needs of both companies, who would contribute complementary resources. The parent companies had spent over two years getting to know each other and negotiating. During that period, each company had invested a substantial amount of money, managerial time and effort via 20 visits and meetings to build a relationship before they decided to negotiate a joint-venture agreement. However, Nora and Sakari could not agree on the terms presented at their final negotiation. Nora, nonetheless, was expected to fulfill TMB's contract soon.

The negotiations had failed to result in an agreement for at least three reasons:

1. Lack of Full Support by the Finns

The management at Sakari had split views on the joint venture. There was internal competition for the company's limited resources from those who wanted to invest in the United Kingdom and eventually penetrate the European market. It was mainly Sakari managers positioned in the Asian regional office who were keen on the joint venture with Nora. They were familiar with the region and had a better understanding of the vast potential in Asia. Although these managers had Sakari's vice-president on their side, there were others who were pushing for the European market and making it difficult for the Asian advocates to obtain full support for their proposal.

On the other hand, the managers in support of the European proposal arguably may have also had a global outlook concerning where to locate Sakari's limited resources. Why should Sakari invest in Asia if similar opportunities were available in Europe? Geographically, Europe is closer to Finland, and presumably, the cultural distance between the Finns and the British is smaller than that between the Finns and the Malays. Consequently, there would be less uncertainty and risk investing in the UK rather than in Malaysia.

2. Lack of Preparation

The Sakari negotiators seemed to lack an awareness of local industry standards when they presented their proposal that included high expatriate salaries. Apparently, they did not make an effort to research the industry rates.

Similarly, the Nora negotiators also seemed to lack understanding of the need for the Sakari negotiators to refer to the head office in Helsinki for further directives. They were also not appreciative of the constraints the Sakari negotiators had to face in defending the joint venture with Nora in view of the split opinion about where Sakari should locate its foreign investments.

3. Lack of Understanding on Differences Due to National Cultures

Although Nora had previous experience in cooperative arrangements, they were unaware that the Finns were so culturally different from other countries. It was a mistake on the part of the Nora negotiators to assume that the Finns were culturally similar to the other western cultures they had dealt with before.

Sakari, whose businesses had been limited to the other Scandinavian countries and Russia, lacked experience dealing with companies from countries such as Malaysia. Although Sakari managers in the Asian regional office were familiar with the local companies, the decision makers in Helsinki were not.

The process of getting to know each partner had been quite lengthy. The long process would arguably indicate the willingness of each partner to spend time and money in building a relationship. On the other hand, it could also reflect that both partners lacked negotiation capabilities or were confronted with difficulties in dealing with each other due to cultural differences. Such differences often delay the development of trust and understanding of each other's needs and potential contribution to the joint venture.

Given this background David, how would you tackle the issue?

Well, based on our earlier discussions, I'd want to start by determining whether formation of a joint venture was the best available alternative.

Exactly. So let's start by looking at the strategic logic.

Nora was motivated to form the joint venture for the purpose of diversifying into a new, related business. The company had been in the telecom industry for more than 10 years but had not ventured into the switching business. In view of the potential profits in this business, Nora has decided they wanted to acquire the switching technology. Although the switching technology could be acquired through a licensing agreement or on the open market, the real learning that results from working and solving problems with personnel from the technology provider is limited with these two options. Thus the joint venture was a better alternative than the alternatives in enabling Nora to achieve its objectives.

The choice of Sakari as a partner was appropriate to Nora because Sakari's switching system would allow the use of standard components available on the open market and the joint venture would not be dependent solely on Sakari for the supply of components. In addition, modular systems are more customer-oriented, a feature which Nora wanted to incorporate in its own switching systems.

Sakari's motivation to form the joint venture was to expand into new markets with its existing switching technology. The South-east Asian market offered a vast potential in view of the lower telephone penetration rates and increased demand for more advanced and sophisticated telecom equipment. However, compared to larger telecom MNCs, Sakari's capabilities in fixed networks were not as well known in this part of the world. Also, Sakari's international activity in the past was limited. Thus Sakari required the assistance of local companies that "know the ropes" in the local scene to enter such new and unfamiliar markets. Although Nora was a private company and had no affiliation with the government, the company had experience in the local telecom industry sufficient to provide local knowledge to the joint venture.

Sakari had a switching technology that was flexible; it could be applied in large telephone exchanges to serve densely populated areas as well as in small exchanges to serve sparsely populated areas. Such technology was quite appropriate for developing countries such as Malaysia, Thailand and Indonesia where switching exchanges could be installed efficiently to serve customers in the cities or in rural areas. The rapid economic growth in these countries was also an indicator that the demand for telecom infrastructure would be high. However, these markets were somewhat "restrictive" because the national governments tend to limit foreign equity participation in certain sectors. Therefore, the choice of entry mode into these markets was limited to licensing and joint venture. Although licensing the technology to Nora was an alternative, a one-time sale was less profitable and Sakari would not be able to acquire the local market knowledge it needed to compete in these markets in the future. Forming a joint venture was the best available alternative to Sakari.

So in sum, there was a sound logic for the JV from both perspectives.

These companies appear to have a very strong logic for joint venturing. Given that, what was the problem?

By the time of this twenty-first meeting between the two potential partners, there were still unresolved issues in five areas (Table 11.1).

The specifics don't matter here. The fact is that in many, many JVs there will be a comparable list of sticking points between the partners. The question is, once you get to this point, what do you do?

Dig in. See if we can figure out how to get them to accept our position.

TABLE 11.1 Unresolved Issues from the Meeting

Issues	Sakari (Finland)	Recommended terms of new deal	Nora (Malaysia)
Equity	51% Nora 49% Sakari		70% Nora 30% Sakari
Technology	JV assembles the switch		JV develops the switch
Royalty	5% of gross sales		2% of net sales
Expatriate salaries	Short-term: US$700/day Long-term: US$12,000 to US$15,000/month		Short-term: RM700/day Long-term: RM12,000 to RM15,000/month
Arbitration location	Helsinki		KL

Note: One RM (Malaysian ringit) was worth less than half of one US dollar.

But isn't that the same approach that both partners have used in their first twenty meetings? What makes you think that this approach will suddenly work?

Okay, so maybe it won't work. So what do you suggest?

Change the way in which you approach negotiations. Currently the people in this negotiation have all had only one overarching decision rule or principle guiding their negotiation approach: how do I get the best possible deal for me.

But isn't this how every negotiation ought to work?

No. This kind of approach may be fine if you are trying to buy t-shirts from a beach vendor you are never going to see again, but it is not enough for any long-term relationship. If you treat each element of a joint venture negotiation as if it was a one-time transaction, you've missed the point.

The objective of any JV negotiation is to resolve the legitimate interests of both partners such that each will be satisfied with the overall outcome. You'll note that this approach has at least three differences from the one you mentioned. First, it acknowledges that each partner has legitimate claims or preferences. It can't necessarily be seen as one partner being right and the other wrong. Second, it acknowledges that two people have to be satisfied, not just one. Otherwise, the JV agreement will either never get signed, or will always possess some inherent instability. Third, the focus is on overall outcome, not "winning" on every individual issue.

Okay, this makes a lot of sense, but I still don't see exactly how you translate this approach into a way of resolving the list of issues that require resolution with the partner.

We do it by jointly developing a set of decision rules that guide how issues will be resolved. There are lots of possible ones available, and ideally these should be discussed and agreed upon before jumping into the specifics. Let me give you some examples of possible decision rules.

> **Decision rules for negotiating effective JVs faster**
>
> 1. What is best for the *actual* JV? (versus best for either partner) Can each partner live with this philosophy?
> 2. What is the standard/common international price or practice?
> 3. Are you adopting a long-term approach, or are you hedging?
> 4. What are the actual issues "to the customers"?
> 5. What are your indifference points?
> 6. Are you leaving sufficient opportunity for profit for your partner?

This is not intended as an exhaustive list, and certainly the partners might not be willing to agree on all of them. But I think you'll agree, none of them are particularly radical or unreasonable.

No, they each seem like reasonable starting points if two partners are serious about developing a joint venture for the long term.

Then, let's apply these particular decision points to the actual unresolved issues.

Okay. Well, if the partners were to use standard international practice, then the arbitration location decision would probably disappear since standard practice is to use a neutral location. Similarly, if the partners were to adopt a decision rule of doing what is best for the actual JV, the royalty paid would be lower than what the Finns are requesting and it would be on net—not gross—sales. Also, the expatriate salaries would be at the lower RM, not US$ levels. This would be in the best interest of the JV's customers, since it would be they who would ultimately have to absorb (via product price) the higher expatriate salaries which would need to be passed on to customers.

So how are we doing so far?

Great. We've taken three of five issues off the table by employing decision rules that my company at least, would have no problem in buying into. That said, there are still two big ones left.

Agreed. But now at least the partners can have a more focused discussion, one that allows them to zero in on the make or break issues. How would you suggest the partners proceed now?

Well, if I go back to the list of potential decision rules, I suspect that the current positions of each side regarding equity and technology are not within the indifference range of the other. I can't imagine that the Malaysians would agree to a JV that merely assembles a switch in exchange for nearly 50% of the equity. And I can't imagine that the Finns would agree to a JV that transfers enough technology for the development of a new switch, in exchange for only 30% of the equity. So I think both sides are going to have to move from their current positions regarding equity and technology. Otherwise there will be no deal.

Agreed. So is there a middle ground possible? Is there a position that would give each partner enough of what they want such that they would be committed to the JV?

I don't know for sure, but I think so. If the Malaysians could somehow see some technology eventually transferred, I suspect they'd be willing to allow the Finns to have a greater equity stake. Similarly, if the Finns could see enough market potential for a newly developed switch—perhaps through regional exports—I suspect they'd be more willing to go for the JV. However, I think they'd still want more than a 30% equity stake.

Congratulations David. You've negotiated a deal in 15 minutes that it took these partners 21 meetings to resolve. And your deal is very close to what they actually did.

The issues were resolved as follows:

- Equity: Nora 60%, Sakari 40%. The joint venture must export its products.
- Technology: The joint venture will assemble the switch for the TMB contract and develop a new switch for export.
- Royalty payments: Three percent on net sales.
- Expatriate payments: Sakari accepted all rates proposed by Nora at the July meeting.
- Location for arbitration: Switzerland.

Hey, this joint venturing isn't so tough. So what do we talk about now?

Nothing. I need to get some sleep.

But I've got some questions I've been saving.

I bet. If I'm awake before the flight lands, maybe we'll have time to get to them. But I really do need some sleep.

PART 5
Operating the JV

12

How Do You Manage Conflict in a JV?

Are you awake yet Peter? Hey Peter, our flight lands in a few hours and I've got some questions.

As Peter reluctantly removed his eyeshades and earplugs and reached for his bottle of water, Lee began his questions.

Peter: The joint venture I'm trying to set up is my first one. Can I expect to see much conflict in it?

You can certainly expect to see some. How much will be mostly up to you and your partner. Because joint ventures consist of three entities—the two parents and the newly created joint venture organization—and these entities will have somewhat different goals and organizational climates, conflict will always exist to some extent. This is especially true in contexts where firms from diverse national and organizational cultures meet.

For an IJV to be successful, it is important for the parties involved to avoid unnecessary conflict. Hopefully, if you've carefully selected your partner and designed things right, there won't be much conflict. This is sort of like choosing between two cars: with one they have a great repair department for this regularly required service. In the other they have only a small repair department because they design and build their vehicle in such a way that repairs are seldom required. Most of us would choose this latter type.

But you can't do away with all conflict can you?

No. Finding ways to avoid conflict is only half of the problem because some conflict is inevitable in all IJVs. The reason some level of conflict is likely in inter-organizational relationships like IJVs is because organizations normally strive to maintain their autonomy even in relationships where they desire cooperation. An optimal way to manage such conflict is therefore also needed. Fortunately, there are some strategies available for managing JV conflict.

That's good to know, but before we consider them, I want to ask a question. Is there a relationship between the amount of conflict and the actual performance of a joint venture? Intuitively, I expect there would be.

You're right. The amount of conflict inversely affects IJV performance. Conflict between parties involved in an IJV also limits success by preventing the venture from being able to accomplish much by blocking decision-making. Such circumstances may also limit an IJV's ability to respond to environmental changes and, thus, to be successful. Conflict may also result in the unwillingness of parent firms to contribute resources that the IJV needs to achieve its goals. Holding back such needed resources would obviously adversely affect IJV performance and survival.

So we should try to eliminate all conflict?

No. A small amount of conflict may be healthy for a joint venture since it may force management to evaluate its decisions more carefully. For example, managers may find after some thought that the other party's plan is superior, or they may simply benefit from refining their plan in the process of thinking more carefully through their plan's logic. Such conflict can be considered constructive conflict.

This is in contrast to the more common destructive conflict. The line of reasoning presented above is in keeping with my central thrust that argues that how one manages conflict is critical so that it has a minimal negative, or perhaps even slightly positive, impact on the JV.

When JV managers are asked if a small amount of conflict was likely to have a positive effect on IJV performance since it would increase the care with which decisions were made, most indicate that a small amount of conflict could have a beneficial effect.

So how would you suggest conflict be managed?

Here are some strategies for minimizing conflict's negative impact, or perhaps even channeling a small amount of conflict into a positive result, which repeatedly emerged from interviews with IJVGMs. We can discuss each in turn.

Strategies for Dealing With JV Conflict

1. Align Partners' Objectives
2. Ensure Adequate Communication between Involved Parties
3. Develop Standard Procedures for Resolving Conflict
4. Don't Only Try to Maximize Your Gain, But Consider the Gain of All Involved Parties
5. Express Understanding of the Other Party's View
6. Empower Locally Based Foreign Managers to Make Most Decisions
7. Develop High Tolerance and Understanding for Different National Cultures
8. Ensure All Parties Are Committed to the IJV
9. Discuss Ways to Avoid Future Conflict

Align Partners' Objectives

Partners involved in a joint venture may well have some different goals. This is quite natural. However, as we talked about earlier, if possible, partners' objectives should be aligned, or congruent, so that achieving one partner's objective will be beneficial for the other as well.

Ensure Adequate Communication between Involved Parties

It is important that parties involved in a conflict find some way to communicate with one another. This communication can help each party understand the other party's view. Understanding can be achieved only through communication. After talking, partner A still may not agree with partner B's view. However, understanding each other's thinking is an important first step in resolving the conflict.

Once this understanding is achieved, communication then serves a second function. At this point communication helps the two parties work out a compromise about their differences. Communication can also help prevent a similar conflict in the future. Parties will generally feel better about the current conflict if they feel assured that the same type of conflict will not recur.

But what if you are in a company that doesn't like to compromise?

Well, if you were unwilling to compromise, once again I'd say you ought to think long and hard about whether you should be in any JV.

Develop Standard Procedures for Resolving Conflict

When conflict exists between two parties, it is much more difficult to negotiate its resolution than it would have been when discussing a hypothetical conflict. Thus, before a conflict develops, it is desirable to develop a standard procedure for resolving conflict. For example, one possible conflict resolution procedure would be to agree that when conflict exists, both parties would talk several times to each other. In such cases each party might prepare a short document explaining why its view seems optimal. If, after the partners read and talk about these documents, no resolution were reached, then the conflict would be sent to a previously agreed arbitrator. Having such a standard conflict resolution procedure in place can ease the problem.

Don't Only Try to Maximize Your Gain, But Consider the Gain of All Involved Parties

It is important that any joint venture is designed such that the actual JV and local parent benefit as much as the foreign parent. If all parties involved in a joint venture are not satisfied, the joint venture is doomed to fail. As we've already discussed, both parties require a continuing incentive to remain in a JV.

Express Understanding of the Other Party's View

Inevitably parents will have differing views on a topic. And, while it is unnecessary for local parents to agree with all views of the foreign parents, it is helpful if a parent can express understanding of the other parent's view and explain the reasoning for their different views. Though this may not alter the fact that a conflict exists, it is helpful to understand why different views exist and to behave as though the other party appreciates one's view.

Do you mean fake it that you care? This sounds like something my wife might accuse me of when she's really frustrated with my absent-mindedness.

I don't think I'm going to get into that one with you, David. Let's consider the other four points.

Empower Locally Based Foreign Managers to Make Most Decisions

It can be very frustrating for a local partner to negotiate with a locally based manager from the foreign partner firm if the foreign partner manager does not have enough authority to make decisions. When a locally derived tentative agreement is deemed unacceptable to management at headquarters, negotiations must start over again. In the second round of negotiations, local partners normally have far less patience—understandably annoyed that the first agreement did not work out—and thus conflict is more likely to develop.

Develop High Tolerance and Understanding for Different National Cultures

Parties must understand that though national cultures and organizational climates are different, none are "the best." They are just different. It is not uncommon for at least some of the people from each partner to possess a somewhat ethnocentric attitude. However, it is also important to remember that traditions normally were developed for a reason. People accustomed to different organizational climates have different expectations. Developing a tolerance for different cultures is helpful to the successful resolution of many conflicts.

Ensure All Parties Are Committed to the IJV

As we've discussed already, all parties need to be committed to a joint venture for the long-term. Joint ventures can yield good results, but they are challenging to make work. It is very difficult to get around the risk/reward tradeoff—that potential for high return leads to high risk. If a parent firm has an attitude of "this would be nice if it works out, but if it does not it is not that important for us," then a conflict can easily derail a joint venture. Parents that are strongly committed to a joint venture for the long-term are more likely to work hard to resolve conflicts that emerge and to exercise restraint that can help prevent and solve conflicts.

Discuss Ways to Avoid Future Conflict

Though conflicts are unfortunate, some conflicts are inevitable. However, if parties involved in a conflict can feel that a similar conflict is unlikely to result in the future as a result of what has been learned, the parties are likely to feel better about the discomfort. In addition, the IJV will benefit from avoiding some future conflicts. As a result, once a conflict is resolved, it is important to discuss why a conflict developed and how similar conflicts can be avoided in the future.

Just then a voice interjected from the seats directly behind Boyd and Lee. These seats had been empty for the first six hours of the flight.

"I've been listening to you guys talk about managing conflict for the last ten minutes and it reminds me of the same garbage I heard from this idiot marriage counselor my third wife dragged me to see. I'm an expert on marriage, seeing as how I'm on my fourth one. And I can tell you, whether it's a marriage or a joint venture, you got to have one person calling all the shots. And if you have any conflict with someone, replace 'em. Get a new partner."

"That is a very interesting perspective," replied Boyd. "Tell me, are you also an expert on joint ventures?"

"You bet. We've got a couple of them in China that I'm in charge of."

"Ah. And how are they doing?"

"Well the partners in both of them are idiots too. So I'm on my way to see if I can sign on some new ones over the next coupla weeks."

At this point, the purser appeared, and approached the man in row 3. "Excuse me sir. May I see your boarding pass?"

"Oh, I'm not in this seat, I just came up here because there's more leg room."

"I'm sorry sir, you're going to have to return to your assigned seat." As he got up to leave, Boyd interjected: "Before you go, could you tell me which company you work for?"

The stranger responded, was escorted away, and Boyd and Lee resumed their discussion.

Geez, Peter. I don't think I'd want to do business with that guy. And it sounds to me like the only thing he's an expert on is divorce. But one thing I'm curious about, why'd you want to know which company he works for?

Simple. I want to short the stock.

13

Learning from IJVs

Peter, I've heard some people talking about the potential of learning from, or with, one's partner in a JV. Can we talk about this?

Sure. Learning through JV activities is both a widely recognized imperative and opportunity. Learning opportunities exist in partnerships that are formed for strategic, operational or financial motivations. While JVs provide learning opportunities and arguments are made for the importance of learning, the use of JVs as major learning vehicles is as yet inconclusive.

How does learning occur?

Lots of ways. These include via expatriates, shared technical systems, socialization, shared R&D, purchase of services from the IJV, and so forth.

How is learning in joint ventures typically viewed?

To date, it has been viewed primarily as a transfer of knowledge between partners and from the partners to the IJV. Partners agree to combine their resources and pass along to the JV what they know. Let me illustrate with a graphic.

96 ▪ *Joint Venturing*

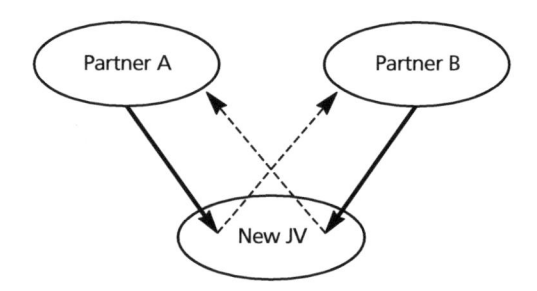

```
    Partner A          Partner B
        \  \         /  /
         \  \       /  /
          \  \     /  /
           \  \   /  /
            \  \ /  /
             \  X  /
              \/ \/
              New JV
```

The dotted line is intended to represent the indirect route by which Partner A and Partner B may learn from each other. Since each of their contributions (the solid line) is intended to benefit the actual new JV, there is not a direct solid line between the two partners.

Any parent company that does make explicit its desire to learn what it's partner knows, about non-JV related issues, would be treated as a potential competitor, rather than partner. This is similar to our earlier discussion about stability: in that it is important to distinguish between the desires to access a partner's knowledge for a JV, as opposed to acquire it.

A second type of possible learning in joint ventures is transformation. Transformation integrates contributed resources and competencies, adapts them to the new context and creates new competencies through the joint activities. The application of contributed resources and competencies to a new context allows for inconsistencies and assumptions to surface that become resolved through transformation.

Finally, harvesting transformed knowledge from the IJV back into the partner firms can enhance other internal or alliance activities that the parent engages in. These enhancements can potentially sustain and improve competitive advantage.

So there is something that parent firms might learn from a joint venture?

Yes. IJVs provide the opportunity for learning both within the IJV and by the parent firms. For the parent however, learning is usually a secondary or tertiary motive and learning opportunities are often unexploited.

Why do parent managers not harvest knowledge from the JV?

Three reasons:

1. No recognition by parent managers of the importance of the new knowledge;
2. Disbelief by the parent managers that the IJV could offer any valuable lessons;

3. The financial performance of the IJV did not convince the parent managers that there was anything worth learning.

Accessing knowledge and learning new skills are secondary motives to market positioning against competitors and sharing risks. The strongest motivation for engaging in an IJV is to access new geographic markets. Those of pre-empting competitors, sharing risks and gaining a strategic hold in competitors' market, follow this motivation closely. Learning new skills or competencies is rated lower.

At the time an IJV is formed, the strongest learning intention is to transfer existing knowledge from the partner to the IJV. The weakest is the intention to harvest knowledge from the IJV to apply to other operations in the firm.

Intent to engage in each type of learning process is significantly related to actual outcomes of that type of learning. In addition, intent to transfer knowledge to and receive knowledge from the partner is correlated, indicating an exchange relationship.

The primary reason firms invest internationally (via wholly owned subsidiary or joint venture) is to increase profits: it is not "to learn." Learning is not a part of the primary strategic logic for most firms when forming JVs.

Then does learning happen in IJVs?

Sometimes yes.

Does such learning improve the JVs performance?

It can, but usually indirectly.

Does the learning that does occur have any value?

Yes. For at least a minority of firms, there are tangible benefits to the corporation, although not necessarily the specific IJV in question.

Are there any companies that are particularly good at learning from joint venturing? Any corporate role models?

Yes. One example that comes to mind immediately is the big pharmaceutical firm: Eli Lilly and Company. In 1999 they even went so far as to establish a separate organizational unit, the Office of Alliance Management (OAM).

The mission of the OAM was to help Lilly develop the alignment, commitment and capabilities needed to achieve each alliance's vision, and to create an environment that would maximize the value of their many alliances. OAM's responsibility in any particular alliance was to serve as the advocate for the collaboration itself. An image of ombudsmen was promoted for the organization. The OAM was also tasked with minimizing the possibility of alliance failure for reasons other than scientific ones, maximizing the value of the partnership, and obtaining more and better alliance opportunities to fuel Lilly's organic growth. The OAM carried the slogan: "We don't make alliances…we make them better."

OAM was also involved in vigorous promotion of the alliance management discipline within the company and promoted its expertise outside the company through industry wide forums such as Association of Strategic Alliance Professionals (ASAP)—an organization comprising a wide range of industry participants with a common interest in creating and disseminating knowledge on alliance management.

Wow. Sounds like they are pretty serious about alliances. How does it actually work?

The company has set up a proprietary process development, using a framework they call the Lilly Alliance Management Process (LAMP). This framework was the outcome of synthesizing best practices from various sources to provide a framework for Lilly to identify common processes and tools to create value through alliances. The graphic that follows lists a sample of management frameworks and tools that were developed by OAM for use in alliance management. These processes, tools, frameworks and approaches were expected to support the alliances as they went through different stages.

For example, the 3-dimensional fit analysis presented a structured way to assess strategic fit, cultural fit and operational fit between the partners. This tool was useful not only for initial analysis of partner fit, but also for monitoring the fit as the alliance evolved, since strategies and leaders often changed within the life of an alliance. Another tool used extensively was the strategic futures exercise, which allowed the partners to articulate what they saw as a future potential for opportunities and problems. It provided a framework for members of the team to present their ideas openly and talk about their concerns.

But who actually runs it?

OAM conceived of three responsibility centers for an alliance: an alliance champion, an alliance leader and an alliance manager. The alliance champion, usually a senior executive, was responsible for high-level support and oversight. Identifying a senior executive as a responsibility center allowed for breaking down the bureaucratic barriers, to facilitate a smooth working relationship. The alliance leader, usually a technical leader or a project manager, was responsible for the day-to-day management of the al-

Learning from IJVs ▪ 99

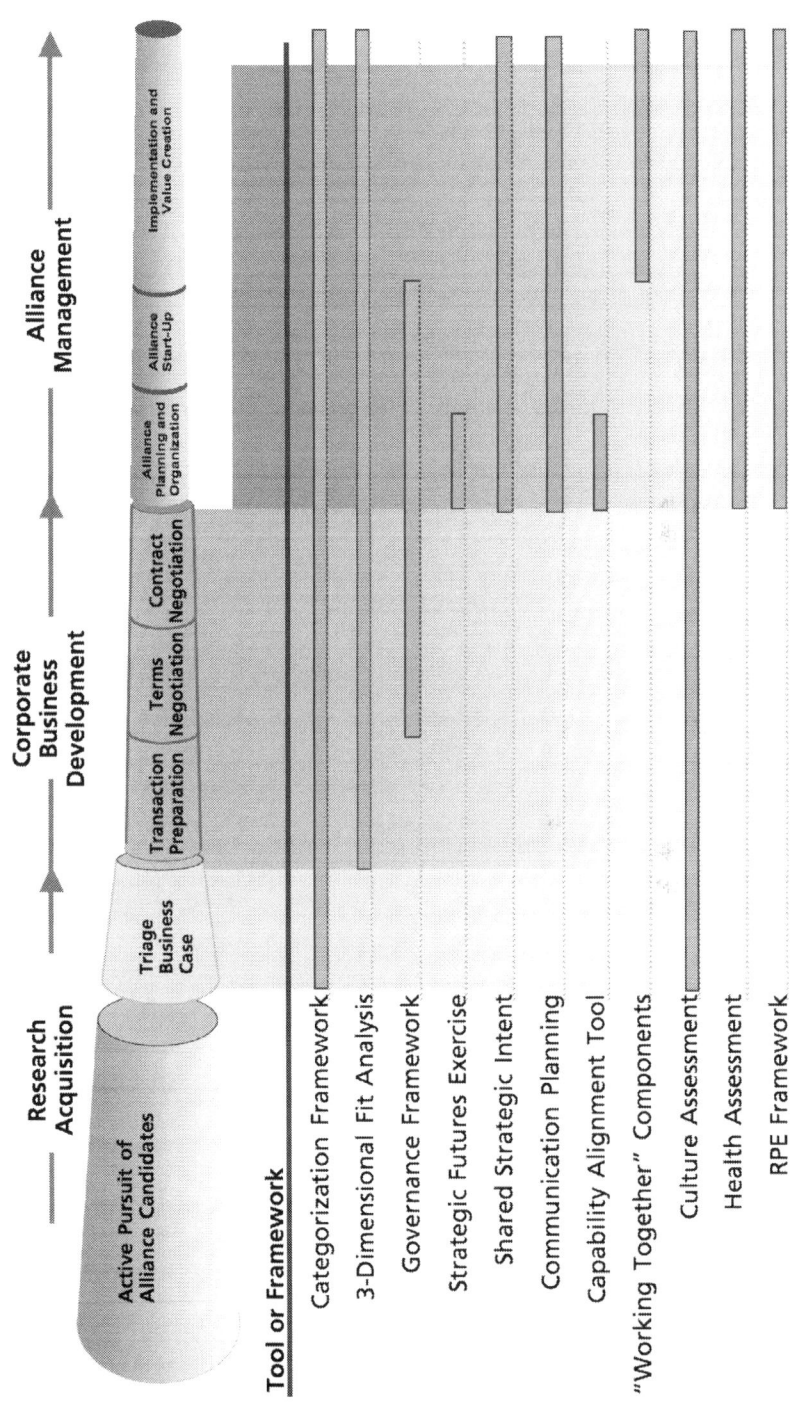

Lilly alliance management process and related tools (examples).

liance and held the line and budget responsibility for the success of the alliance. The alliance manager represented the OAM and served as a business integrator between the two alliance partners. Since alliance managers had the opportunity of seeing through the full cycle of the partnership, they were also instrumental in recommending improvements to the LAMP process.

The alliance manager's responsibilities were broadly in four areas: (1) To provide pre-deal assessment for potential alliances, (2) to facilitate the start-up of new alliances, (3) to support value creation efforts for ongoing and transitioning alliances and (4) to build Lilly's capacity and capability for alliances. When the research acquisition department proposed a potential alliance, alliance managers advised the deal-making team of the potential risks, issues and opportunities, recognizing the impact of the potential deal on existing alliances. The alliance manager participated in the due diligence process, which often included site visits. If the potential alliance passed the due diligence, the alliance manager played an advisory role to the deal-making group, particularly in the area of designing the governance.

Early stage support for new alliances demanded intensive engagement of the alliance manager. In this stage, alliance managers were committed to facilitating alliance meetings whenever necessary, and setting up the governance structure and communication processes at various levels. They played a pivotal role in orchestrating kick-off meetings and engaging alliance personnel from both sides (both Lilly and the partner) in team-building exercises. In supporting ongoing and transitioning alliances, alliance managers served to monitor governance and informal interactions, conducting annual surveys and presenting the data analysis to the team members. Where needed, they also got involved in individual and team interventions to improve alliance health. If any alliance relationship needed to be restructured or terminated, alliance managers were responsible for ensuring the transition progressed as smoothly as possible by playing a catalytic role in the restructuring process.

Peter: This all sounds pretty detailed and complicated. Surely no company—even big ones—have got so many alliances or JVs that it is worth the effort of setting up a specialized structure like this?

Well David, I'm afraid you'd be making a mistake if you assumed this. Most MNE managers not only do not have any idea about how many alliances and JVs they have, but nearly all of them grossly underestimate the corporate totals. Some years ago, I was teaching a module on JVs as part of a training program for a Fortune 500 bank. I asked the 40 bank executives in the room to jot down on a piece of paper how many alliances/JVs they thought the bank was engaged in, and the names of any of those they were familiar with. Everybody knew of between 1 and 5 ventures, and no one estimated more than a dozen in total. When we tallied up the totals, they were stunned to discover that there were 53 separate alliances. Think about the learning opportunities David.

14

Liability of Reorganization

Peter: *After I've been operating my joint venture for a few years, if it runs into problems, I assume that one of the most logical things I can do is redo the equity split, right?*

Well, conventional wisdom certainly has assumed that some sort of organizational change would be feasible and beneficial under such circumstances.

Don't lots of firms redo the equity split over the life of their JV?

A fair number, yes. About one-third of the time, the partners in a joint venture will agree to restructure the ownership levels sometime after it has been formed.

Post-formation IJV structural change

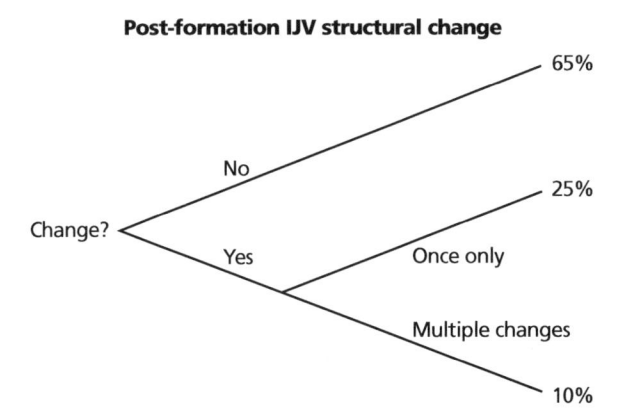

```
                              ── 65%
                   No ──────
                              ── 25%
Change? ──                Once only
                   Yes ──
                           Multiple changes
                              ── 10%
```

Is it easy to do?

Not necessarily. Most JV agreements do not provide an option for one partner or the other to automatically increase their equity holding at the expense of the other. A new equity sharing requires a new negotiation.

Right. I see that in about 10% of JVs, the equity arrangements are actually changed more than once. Are these the best companies, given that they spend more time getting the alignment right?

Certainly one might be tempted to think so. Because fitting organizational structures to environmental or contextual contingencies usually results in high performance, organizations attempt to find a fit by changing organizational structures and adopting new ones that correspond to new conditions as a means for increasing IJV performance and the probability of survival.

I hear some hesitancy in your voice. Why do I have this feeling that you don't think a lot of restructuring is a good idea, that "conventional wisdom" might be wrong?

It is more than hesitancy. Organizational changes can evoke substantive risks. Change can disrupt, hampering an organization's chance of survival. Thus, even if IJV partners undertake a potentially beneficial change of content, benefits might not necessarily be realized because the process of change itself can be so disruptive and deleterious, thereby negatively affecting an organization's performance and survival.

What would cause this?

This disruption is attributable to what I would call a liability of reorganization; that is, the likelihood that higher failure rates will occur among IJVs where the equity structure is changed. Here change would essentially set you back to the liability of newness stage by damaging the value of accumulated resources and experience.

You mean too much change is bad?

Exactly. Have a look at this graphic on the impact of structural change on JV performance. The likelihood of failure of IJVs without a structural change initially increases but then eventually declines over time. In contrast, the likelihood of failure of IJVs *with* structural changes continually escalates as the number of structural changes increases.

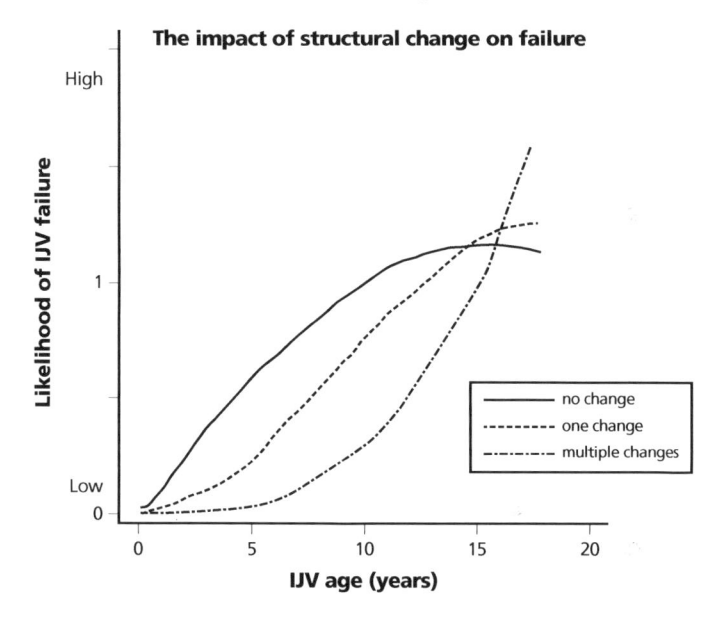

The impact of structural change on failure

Interesting. But it also appears that at least for a few years, reorganization(s) can delay failure. Am I interpreting this properly?

Yes you are David. It is a classic short-term versus long-term phenomena. You can see that by the time the JV investment is about 15 years old, the failure rates are going in very different directions. The likelihood of failure of a JV that has had no organization changes has started to actually decline while those that have had organizational changes are seeing ever increasing failure rates.

Okay. I think I've got it. But what would cause this "liability of reorganization"?

I don't know all the reasons, but can think of a variety of potentially contributing factors. First, a change in structure typically sends a signal that something is amiss, that something requires fixing. When this happens once, many observers and internal managers may give you the benefit of the doubt and view it simply as an adjustment. Do it twice though, and no one will give you the benefit of the doubt: they'll see a negative pattern.

Second, some observers and managers will not give you the benefit of the doubt even the first change. Recall that the norm in most joint ventures is no change in the equity split. Thus to some people, any change can start to create a crisis in confidence. Questions start getting asked: Do we have the right partner? Are the right people managing the JV? Are we in the right market? Are we on a slippery slope of performance decline, so should exit now? All of these questions can contribute to a sort of mid-life crisis for the JV. This can result in over-reaction, and a downward spiral of ownership changes.

Third, I know a lot of experienced managers who have been through multiple reorganizations during their careers and have come to the conclusion that many reorganizations are initiated by executives who haven't taken the time or aren't smart enough to figure out the real root cause of an organization's problem. Either that, or the executives lack the courage to directly confront a problem, so they address the problem by reorganizing everything.

Fourth, a reorganized joint venture in which the partners are spending their time jockeying and negotiating with each other rather than focusing on the JV's external competitors, creates problems. Losing sight of what your competitors are doing is always a bad idea.

It sounds like I better think long and hard about whether I should try to ever change the equity structure in my JV.

I would.

15

Intended and Unintended Termination of Joint Ventures

Peter: *As you can tell, I'm pretty excited about the prospect of not only launching my first joint venture, but also successfully operating it. But contrary to how it might seem, I'm not so naïve as to believe that it couldn't eventually fail. So, I have some questions about failure. Is failure always bad? Isn't it possible that a JV could be intentionally terminated?*

David: These are all good questions, so let's start with JV termination. It can be defined in two ways: the suspension of the structure or the suspension of the existing business domain of the JV (see Figure 15.1). The suspension of the structure represents the transformation from a shared ownership mode to a different organizational mode, such as licensing or a wholly owned subsidiary (WOS). The suspension of the existing business domain of a JV involves either discontinuity or changes in the JV's strategies, core business processes, or key products and markets.

The suspension of the JV structure and business domain may or may not occur concurrently. For example, a JV may transform its organizational

108 ▪ *Joint Venturing*

		Business Domain	
		Sustained	**Suspended**
JV Structure	**Sustained**	Survival	***Instability*** Discontinuity/changes in the strategies, core business processes, or key products and markets of the JV
	Suspended	***Mode change*** JV → licensing JV → WOS	***Complete termination*** (intended and unintended)

Figure 15.1 JV termination classification.

form from a shared ownership mode to an arm's-length contractual mode such as licensing or to a sole ownership mode (a wholly owned subsidiary) but retain its existing business domain. A JV may also suspend or change its existing business domain but maintain the shared ownership structure. The former is referred to as a "mode change" and the latter as instability. My definition of JV termination includes the suspension of both JV structure and business domain, which I term "complete termination," and I further divide it into the categories of intended and unintended termination.

Can you go into a little more detail about what you mean by Intended versus Unintended Termination? I'm a little fuzzy.

The intended termination perspective suggests that JVs are formed for specific purposes, and that their termination occurs when these initial purposes of formation have either been achieved or lost. In contrast, the unintended termination perspective suggests that termination occurs because of unanticipated contingencies that emerge after the formation of the JV. The intended termination perspective says that termination is the mirror image of formation, and can be explained by reversing the logic of JV formation. In contrast, the unintended termination perspective says that JV termination occurs independently of the achievement of the initial purposes of formation, and is explained by more than the reversal of the logic of formation.

The second difference between the two perspectives is how they conceive of success. The intended termination perspective views termination as a positive consequence of joint operations, because it often follows the successful completion of the planned project. In contrast, the unintended termination perspective sees termination as a negative consequence of joint operations, because it often follows the failure of the planned project. The distinction between these perspectives opens up the broader issue of whether a JV should be viewed as an integrated part of a parent firm that is expected to achieve the objectives of the firm, or as a stand alone organization that is evaluated primarily according to financial performance, and for which survival is a pre-condition of its operation.

The third difference is that the two perspectives differ in their implications for the practical management of JVs. The intended termination perspective sees the greater longevity of a JV as a desirable outcome, whereas the unintended termination perspective sees it as an undesirable outcome. As managers act according to the outcome that they desire, their perspectives on termination may lead to different courses of action. If decision makers consider a greater longevity to be a desirable outcome, then they will take action to increase the likelihood that the JV will survive. However, the chosen action may not always be the optimal solution for achieving the initial purposes of formation.

But can't termination occur at different stages and for different reasons?

Yes. Termination can occur before, upon, or after the achievement of the initial purposes of formation. Figure 15.2 shows the various cases of termination. Case 1 represents unintended termination before the achievement of the initial purposes of formation, Case 2 represents intended termination upon the achievement of the initial purposes of formation, and

Case 1	Case 2	Case 3
Unintended termination: Termination occurs before the achievement of the initial purposes of JV formation.	Intended termination: Termination occurs upon the achievement of the initial purposes of JV formation.	Unintended termination: Termination occurs after the achievement of the initial purposes of JV formation.

JV formation →

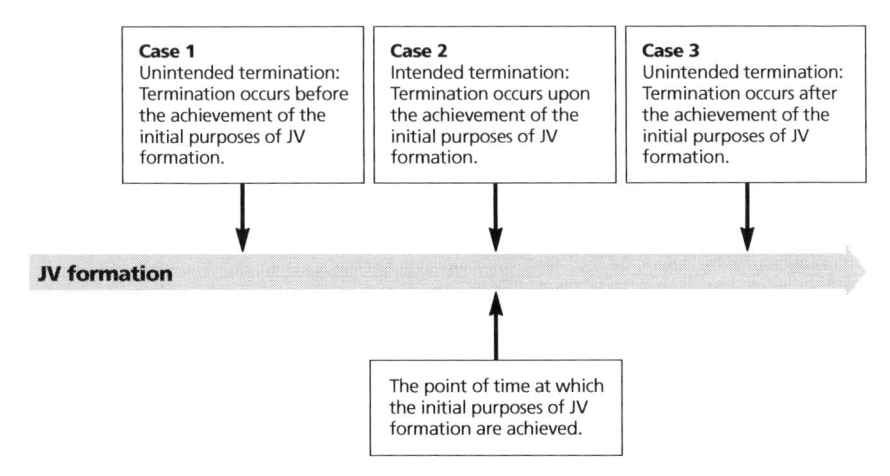

The point of time at which the initial purposes of JV formation are achieved.

Figure 15.2   Termination at various times.

Case 3 represents unintended termination after the achievement of the initial purposes of formation. The difference between Case 2 and Case 3 demonstrates the different view of JV survival. The intended termination perspective suggests that a JV survives because it has reasons (the initial purposes of formation) to continue to operate, at least until the initial purposes of formation have been achieved. In contrast, the unintended termination perspective suggests that a JV survives because it has no reason to suspend its operation, even after the achievement of the initial purposes of formation, unless it encounters unanticipated critical contingencies. The former perspective conceives of survival as a purposive act that aims to attain the specific goals that were initially set for the project, whereas the latter perspective conceives of survival as a default state with an option of termination or further development during the post-formation stage.

As we've already discussed, there are three major stages of JV development (formation, post-formation, or termination). Termination is linked to both the formation and post-formation stages (or the middle stage in the life cycle) of JVs. Termination is closely linked with formation because JVs may be terminated due to the decline, achievement, or loss of the initial purposes of their formation (intended termination). JV termination is also closely linked to post-formation because JVs may be terminated due to unanticipated contingencies that were not present at the time of formation (unintended termination).

When most people think about the link between formation and termination, they implicitly assume that a typical JV is formed to achieve a specific objective, and that it will be more likely to be terminated when it has achieved its initial objective.

But doesn't termination depend at least in part on the original objective of the JV?

Absolutely! As we have already discussed, JVs are formed for a variety of specific objectives, which can generally be classified into four broad purposes. These include access to natural resources and labor (resource/labor seeking), access to locally available financial resources (capital seeking), access to local markets (market seeking), and access to know-how and technology (strategic asset seeking) in the host country. The relative effects of these purposes on both the likelihood of intended termination and the longevity of a JV, however, are dependent on the type of assets that foreign firms are attempting to access through the formation of the JV. Natural resources, labor, capital, and markets are available to—and can readily be accessed by—any investing firms, as long as they are operating in the host country. These assets constitute the comparative advantages of the host country. Foreign firms that seek these assets tend to have a persistent commitment to maintain their JVs, because they can benefit from the comparative advantages of these assets in the host country only as long as their JVs continue to operate there. Under this condition, foreign firms are likely to view the survival of JVs as a default state, and to consider a greater longevity to be a desirable outcome. Therefore, JVs that are formed for the purposes of resource/labor seeking, capital seeking, and market seeking are less likely to be terminated for intended reasons, because the reasons for maintaining their operation are sustained unless the host country loses the comparative advantages of its country-specific assets, which rarely occurs in a short time.

In contrast, strategic assets are more firm-specific in nature, and are possessed only by particular firms in a host country. When JVs are formed for reasons of seeking strategic assets, foreign firms have no reason to maintain them once they have successfully acquired these assets from their local partners, unless there are other strategic asset-seeking opportunities that may be obtained from the same partners. Under this condition, foreign firms tend to view the survival of JVs as lead-time for the achievement of the initial purposes of JV formation, and to consider a lesser longevity to be a desirable outcome. Therefore, JVs that are formed for strategic asset seeking are more likely to be terminated for intended reasons, because the reasons for maintaining them disappear as soon as the relevant strategic assets are acquired from the local partners. Building on this logic, JVs that are formed to seek resources/labor, capital, or markets are less likely to be terminated for intended reasons and to be maintained for longer than those that are formed to seek strategic assets. This is because the former are formed to gain the benefits of the endowments of the host country, which are long lasting, and the latter are more susceptible to the completion of the acquisition of the strategic assets, which are in limited supply.

There must still be a lot of unanticipated reasons for JV failure though, wouldn't there be?

Yes. Unanticipated contingencies span a wide variety of factors in the parent firm, inter-partner, and external environments. These include changes in the conditions of the parent firms, such as the imposition of the corporate policies on foreign operations; changes in the relationship between partners, such as bargaining power, the dilution of trust, inter-partner conflicts, adaptive and conflict resolution mechanisms, and the social ties between partners; and changes in external conditions, such as government regulations, industry concentration and market growth, and home country competition. These types of unanticipated contingencies may influence the longevity of JVs.

Of the three types of unanticipated contingencies, changes in the interpartner relationship are specific to JVs, whereas changes in the parent firm conditions and external conditions are common occurrences that affect both JVs and WOSs. We therefore expect JVs to have a greater likelihood of unintended termination than WOSs, because JVs bear the additional risk of termination that is caused by conflicts and difficulties in the coordination between partners.

The initial conditions under which JVs are formed involve the structural characteristics of the JV partnership and the specific characteristics of the parent firms, which determine the subsequent exchange relationship between the partners, and the institutional conditions that are imprinted on the JV at birth. The influence of the initial conditions tends to persist for a long time over subsequent organizational structures and processes, and becomes a source of organizational inertia, which makes JVs rigid in the face of changes to internal and external conditions during the post-formation stage.

Peter: This is all very interesting, but frankly, a bit abstract. Can you be more specific and just tell me what works?

Sure. Strategic asset seeking JVs have quite a high rate of intended termination (nearly 30%), whereas the resource/labor, market, and capital seeking JVs have a relatively low rate of termination (under 10% each). Further, strategic asset seeking JVs have a much higher rate of intended termination (28.6%) than the strategic asset seeking WOSs (3.2%), which suggests that foreign firms tend to acquire strategic assets more successfully through JV formation than through self-development in a host country.

Resource/labor and market seeking JVs have a greater average longevity than strategic asset seeking JVs.

JVs that are terminated because of misleading demand and conflicts with local partners tend to have a higher likelihood of being terminated before the achievement of the initial purposes of formation (Case 1 in Figure 15.2) and a lesser longevity than those that are terminated because of changes in the parent firm conditions (internal factors).

The majority of the JV termination cases are unintended, and occur due to the emergence of unanticipated contingencies. Most of the unintended JV termination occurred due to changes in external conditions, such as misleading demand (43.1%), competition with local firms (17.1%), and competition with third country firms (10.1%); followed by changes in the inter-partner relationship, such as conflicts with local partners (8.7%); and much less by changes in the parent firm conditions, such as the restructuring of parent firm businesses (2.3%) and the death or retirement of the Japanese CEO (1.2%).

Cultural distance has a significant and negative impact on the longevity of JVs. JV size has a positive and significant impact on the longevity of JVs and international experience has a negative and significant impact on the longevity of JVs.

Intended termination is closely associated with the initial purposes of JV formation, because it occurs upon the achievement of these purposes. Unintended termination occurs due to unanticipated contingencies that emerge after the formation of JVs. Simply reversing the logic of JV formation fails to fully explain JV termination. Most JVs are terminated because of unanticipated contingencies, rather than because the initial purposes of formation had been achieved or had disappeared.

So JV termination should be considered a business failure?

Generally yes. Thus JV managers should establish mechanisms by which to deal with unanticipated contingencies to minimize the chance of unintended termination, given that it is very costly to terminate established IJVs, especially before they have achieved the purposes of their formation.

Not all types of unanticipated contingencies have an equal influence on the longevity of foreign subsidiaries. Changes in external conditions (misleading demand and competition with other firms) are the most critical types of unanticipated contingencies, as they account for over 70% of the total terminated JV cases and about 70% of the total terminated WOS cases. This not only indicates the importance of understanding and adapting to the local environment in the host country, but also suggests that changes in external conditions are the generic causes of unintended termination for all types of foreign subsidiaries, irrespective of whether they are formed as JVs or WOSs. However, changes in the inter-partner relationship are specific to JVs, and thus JVs have a higher likelihood of unintended termination that is due to conflicts with local partners than WOSs. JVs that are terminated due to conflicts with local partners also have a lesser average longevity than those that were terminated due to the achievement of the initial purposes of formation.

Both the rate of termination and the longevity of the JVs vary noticeably across the four main purposes of JV formation. Most noticeably, JVs that are formed for strategic asset seeking purposes tend to have a higher likelihood of intended termination but a lesser longevity than those that formed for the purposes of resource/labor, capital, and market seeking. Thus termination decisions may be contingent on the initial purposes of formation. Strategic asset seeking JVs formulate strategies that facilitate intended termination because a lesser longevity is desired, whereas resource/labor, market, and capital seeking JVs formulate strategies that avoid unintended termination because a greater longevity is desired. Hence, JVs that take very distinct courses of action vary significantly in their likelihood of being intentionally and unintentionally terminated.

In terms of the effects of the initial conditions under which JVs are formed on their longevity, cultural distance between JV partners represents a source of misunderstanding and miscommunication, and smaller JVs tend to have a greater liability.

PART 6

I Still Have a Few Questions…

16

Ideal Number of Partners?

Peter: *We've been talking about a joint venture between two partners. Is it true that many firms enter into partnerships that involve three, four, and five or more firms?*

Yes. A high percentage of equity joint ventures have more than two, or what we can call, multiple partners. In some of these however, some of the partners will have quite a small equity position and behave more like silent investors than active participants in the operation of the business.

Although we have only two partners in our joint venture, there was some discussion early on about having a third partner. Is there a relationship between the number of JV partners and performance? I guess what I'm really asking is whether there is an ideal number of partners in a joint venture?

There are two schools of thought on this issue. One suggests having more partners would be bad; the other that more partners would be good.

Why would performance decrease as the number of partners in a JV increases?

As the number of partners increases, there is potentially a geometric growth in complexity. As the number of inter-partner contacts increase, so do coordination costs, the level of inaccurate information, the degree of managerial complexity, and the number of disagreements, monitoring costs, and the chance of dysfunctional pairings.

As we've already discussed, the search for and choice of the right partner can be a costly undertaking. All else equal, the costs associated with forming a JV with more than one partner would increase. Using similar logic, it seems natural that in a multi-partner JV, the costs associated with monitoring and coordination would also be higher.

Why?

Monitoring costs would be higher in a multi-partner JV than in one with fewer partners because the propensity for firms to act in a self-interested manner is greater. Here it is more difficult to allocate responsibility for whoever it might be that is shirking in their contributions to the JV. Also, when ownership is not equally distributed, partners with a smaller relative equity ownership position would have a much larger incentive to cheat because they stand to gain more than they can lose. Therefore if ownership holdings are smaller, as the number of partners in a JV increases, the overall incentive to cheat should increase, because the absolute value of ownership of each partner is decreasing.

If JVs allow partners to access and trade people, facilities, documents, knowledge and other resources, then cheating will occur when access is denied or the value of the various trades are unequal. Multi-partner JVs would be more prone to learning races as they offer more opportunities to share resources.

What are learning races?

As we discussed earlier, in a small number of JVs, a partner's objective might be to acquire what the other(s) know, rather than be satisfied with access.

To avoid learning races, which always eventually result in the termination of the JV, partners must invest in complex monitoring and coordination mechanisms, thus driving up the operating costs of multi-partner JVs.

But can't some of this be managed?

Yes. While one can make a strong argument on the cost side for why multi-partner JVs might perform more poorly than those with fewer partners, the magnitude of these costs may not necessarily be great. First, in a multi-partner JV, the payoff from cheating is unclear. Here even a strong self-orientation is not necessarily associated with increased individual benefits. Second, the successful operation of multi-partner JVs depends on access to each partner's resources for survival. Cooperative, rather than competitive behavior between partners should engender trust in each partner's competence, dependability and resources, which should decrease monitoring costs. Third, JV learning races are rare. Fewer than 5% of all JVs are formed with the objective of learning what the partner knows so you can dump them. Over 95% of JVs were formed to make money for the partners by matching their complementary skills. They are not short-lived and unstable, typical of JVs formed for learning race purposes. Finally, because shared ownership means that all owners share negotiating and monitoring costs associated with opportunistic behavior, partners are similar to what some economists call "mutual hostages" and less inclined to act opportunistically.

Although the costs of opportunism may not be clearly prevalent in multi-partner JVs, the costs associated with the process of exchange itself, can also become complex here. Successful integration and contracting in a multi-partner venture requires a greater need for communication via mechanisms like meetings and personal contacts. These mechanisms are costly and increase the coordination costs. However, the increased coordination costs are not necessarily a negative. In fact trust, cooperative behavior and a team perspective can create an environment whereby partners of the multi-partner JV naturally meld their own individual interests with the interests of the group. To achieve this they rely less on expensive tangible coordination mechanisms and more on socialization.

So how does the argument go as to why performance would increase as the number of partners in a JV increases?

Multi-partner JVs should earn greater returns than two partner JVs because, firstly, they benefit from the environmental scanning abilities and managerial expertise of all partners, thus allowing them to identify and deal with a greater number of potential opportunities and threats. Secondly, resource development in a multi-partner JV is more complex, thus resulting in competitive advantages that are more sustainable and less easily imitated. Thirdly, multi-partner JVs have immediate access to more diverse resources as partners draw from distinctly different resource pools, thus increasing the potential for synergy from integration. This diversity is increased when partners come from different countries. The link between complexity and competitive advantage for international multi-partner JVs originates in the varied sources of resource contribution. The assumption is that, all else equal, multiple partners and cultural distance between partners are positively linked to resource diversity and that in turn, this diversity will add value to the JV. Resource diversity refers to different, complementary capabilities that help the organization create value. We can assume that diversity within firms comes from differences in resource positions. Therefore, as the number of partners increases, the technical, managerial and financial variety of resources, may also increase.

So what is the net result of these two opposing perspectives?

Performance is fairly invariant to the number of partners. Further, this relationship is no clearer by region. As well, if the phenomena are split out by the sector in which the subsidiary operates (services or manufacturing), there is again no significant trend.

So the number of partners is not necessarily important?

Number of partners is neither a significant nor substantive predictor of JV performance.

Hmm. What do you know. I'd always thought that having a bunch of partners was a bad thing.

You certainly aren't alone with that attitude. Most discussion on partner selection focuses on the importance of the quality of partners on JV success and/or failure, saying little about the impact of the quantity of partners. In fact, it assumes that as the number of partners in a JV increases, the probability that it will achieve high levels of performance decreases.

A lot of managers have typically assumed a negative influence of too many partners on JV performance. The resulting implications for managers was thus a prevailing attitude where they would beware of participating in multi-partner joint ventures, as they felt the potential managerial inefficiencies, decision-making complexities, and overall decrease in the speed of decision making would put future performance at risk.

However, in fact, the number of partners by itself does not seem to affect firm performance. In today's business environment, opportunities are complex and in order to take advantage of these opportunities, firms are often required to collaborate with more than one player from the same and/or different industries. Managers biased by the assumption that multi-partner joint ventures tend to perform poorly, are less likely to be able to take advantage of these opportunities.

So let me see if I can summarize. There is no clear relationship between number of partners and firm performance. When deciding to form a JV, we should focus primarily on the quality of partners and not be dissuaded from considering more than one partner due to the risk of decreased performance.

That's it.

17

JVs with Small- and Medium-Sized Enterprises (SMEs)

One *of my neighbours back home was telling me, Peter, that he is in a joint venture. But he has a small company. Is there any difference between JVs in big versus small companies?*

A growing number of international joint ventures involve small and medium enterprises. Yet, the focus of most discussion tends to be on IJVs established by large firms. Compared to large firms, small and medium sized enterprises (what we call SMEs) have limited financial and managerial resources. Further, SMEs are usually owned and managed by founders, whereas large firms are managed by professionals. As a result, the decision-making in SMEs is highly centralized. Entrepreneurs/owners of SMEs are less comprehensive in their decision behaviour as compared to large firms' professional managers. Such behaviours have a negative impact on SME performance.

You aren't suggesting that the people running SMEs aren't as smart as those in large firms are you?

No, not at all. In fact, some of the people running small firms are among the brightest folks I've ever met. What I am saying though is that entrepreneurs/owners are typically drawing from the experiences/expertise of a smaller group of people, which in turn can hurt performance.

How important are joint ventures for SMEs as they internationalize?

They are especially important for SMEs in their internationalization process. By definition, SMEs have more constraints in resources and capabilities as compared to large firms. As a result, SMEs are subject to a liability of smallness which is reflected in their difficulties in obtaining and securing critical resources such as capital and staff, and their vulnerability to environmental changes. Such disadvantages impose constraints on the expansion of small and medium enterprises both in the domestic market and international markets. In fact, the liability of smallness can be "hereditary" and can adversely affect the future of SMEs' subsidiaries. As "children" of SME parents, SMEs' subsidiaries tend to be small in size and are subject to the same set of constraints in resources and capabilities that confront the SME parents. For SMEs' overseas subsidiaries, the liability of smallness inflates the liabilities of foreignness, newness, and relational orientation.

There are four of these so-called "liabilities" facing small companies?

Yes. Foreign subsidiaries of all firms, large or small, face liabilities, when the target markets are new to the parent firms and when they are greenfield investments that involve the establishment of new subsidiaries (instead of brownfield investments such as acquisitions). The liability of foreignness places foreign subsidiaries in a disadvantageous position in competition with local firms who are familiar with the local environment and have established good local connections. All overseas subsidiaries face this problem, but it can be a more severe problem for SMEs because they are less experienced in international markets compared to large firms.

How does the liability of newness work?

The liability of newness is reflected in the series of operational challenges facing a start-up, such as financing, recruiting, procuring and marketing. More importantly, the liability of newness raises the issue of legitimacy which directly affects the solution to all the above operational challenges. Compared to incumbents, new entrants have to work hard to prove themselves in order to establish relationships with various stakeholders. The legitimizing process can be both expensive and time-consuming, substantially increasing the challenges faced by the new subsidiaries. This process can be more difficult for SMEs' new subsidiaries because they can not leverage their SME parents' public awareness as can the new subsidiaries by large firms who are more well-known.

What is a liability of relational orientation?

The liability of relational orientation relates to the fact that many entrepreneurs achieved initial success because of their single-minded pursuit of objectives. Those with a do-it-themselves (wholly owned) rather than a relational (cooperative) orientation, may have difficulty making joint ventures work.

So how do the small companies overcome their problem of limited resources?

Resources of particular interest to SMEs in their international expansion are knowledge about the local markets, firm reputation and financial capital. IJV partners' knowledge about the local markets can help reduce the liability of foreignness confronted by SMEs' foreign subsidiaries. IJV partners' knowledge about the local markets depends on the partners' experience in the local markets. IJV partners' reputation provides endorsement to SMEs' foreign subsidiaries and thus helps mitigate their liabilities of newness. IJV partners' financial capital can alleviate the financial constraints of SMEs' foreign subsidiaries and help reduce their liabilities of smallness. IJV partners' reputation and financial capital are closely associated with the size of the partners.

Is it possible for small and medium-sized enterprises to acquire local knowledge and develop new organizational capabilities internally through incremental experience accumulation in new markets?

Yes. However, this learning-by-doing process takes time and can result in mistakes. Coupled with the vulnerability as a result of their small size, these mistakes can endanger the longevity of both SME's foreign subsidiaries and their SME parents. By accessing an IJV partners' local knowledge base, an SME's foreign subsidiary can expedite its learning process and minimize mistakes.

A local (host country) partner represents a primary source of local knowledge as compared to home country partners. As we've already discussed, a local partner tends to have more detailed knowledge about various aspects of the host country environment, as compared to the other partner options. A local firm is familiar with the needs and tastes of the local consumers. It has information about local competitors. It also has local networks that can provide its international joint venture(s) with timely information on the changes in the local environment.

While a local partner can contribute to superior IJV performance through the reduction in the liability of foreignness, its value can depreciate over the life cycle of the international joint venture. As foreign partners accumulate experience in the local environment, they become less dependent on local partners for local knowledge and some even find that the role of local partner is redundant. As the dependence on a local partner's local knowledge decreases, a foreign partner's bargaining power over the local partner increases. The change in the balance of the bargaining power between local and foreign partners can lead to IJV instability or even IJV dissolution.

What can a large firm gain by seeking out a foreign SME as a partner?

All the usual things: a new technology, a new process, market or product knowledge, and so forth. Partnering with small firms may help the large firms stay at the forefront of innovation. All of these potential contributions may not necessarily exist in larger potential foreign partners, or such partnering may jeopardize some other relationship which they already have.

What can a small firm gain by joint venturing with a large firm?

As I've already mentioned, there are a number of contributions that large firms can bring to SMEs' foreign subsidiaries. Two of the most critical are resources and reputation. By definition, large firms are more resource rich. With the resource backup from large firms, SMEs' foreign subsidiaries can achieve full operation and growth faster than otherwise would be possible with the resource constraints of SMEs. As the international joint ventures grow, they accumulate greater managerial and financial resources themselves and become less vulnerable. The situation is likely to enhance IJV longevity.

In addition, partnering with large firms also allows small and medium enterprises to leverage the reputations of large firms to more quickly establish the legitimacy of their international joint ventures in host countries. Large size tends to legitimate organizations, to the extent that large size is interpreted by external stakeholders as an outcome of an organization's prior success. Business connections with large firms, either in the form of one-term business transactions or long-term partnership, enhance the legitimacy of smaller firms. In a similar vein, with large firms as a partner in the international joint venture, SMEs' international joint ventures can shorten the time it takes to establish legitimacy in the relevant industries and host countries. With the establishment of their legitimacy and enhanced visibility and image, it is easier for SMEs' international joint ventures to obtain financial and human resources in local markets and develop local networks with suppliers and buyers.

In addition, large partners have resources and incentives to keep their subsidiaries operating. With "deep pockets," large firms can better sustain losses from some of their subsidiaries. Large firms may also have a longer-term view towards foreign investments, allowing them to keep their subsidiaries operating a bit longer to assess their viability. Further, social considerations may also permit large firms to maintain their subsidiaries, even if they are incurring losses. Large firms tend to attract disproportionate attention from the public. Large firms are arguably more concerned than small and medium enterprises about the downside effect on their reputation associated with the dissolution of their international joint ventures. To maintain favorable public image, large firms may hesitate from quickly terminating unprofitable subsidiaries. All factors, from either economic or social perspectives, point to an increase in the longevity of international joint ventures with large partners.

Do large firms exploit their position of power?

Although large firms are in a position to exploit SME partners in their joint ventures, the extent that exploitation by large partners happens depends on the level of equity ownership of large partners in the IJVs. To some extent, equity positions are like "hostages" or "collaterals" which can help ease opportunism in joint ventures. Therefore, as large partners' equity levels in IJVs increase to a significant or perhaps even a majority (51%+) equity position, there is no real incentive for them to exploit the IJVs and their smaller partners.

When small firms look for a JV partner for doing business in another country, should they look to the local country (the one they are investing in) or to their own home country?

The use of a local partner has positive impacts on the profitability of SMEs' IJVs. Both local partners and home country partners are viable sources of local knowledge. However, for small and medium enterprises, local partners seem to be a more effective choice than home country partners for access to local knowledge. The positive effects that a local partner has on an IJV's profitability highlight the importance of local knowledge and the fact that a local partner presents a primary source of local knowledge.

What is the impact of having this local knowledge on the JV's longevity?

Host country knowledge, either from local partners or foreign partners, has a strong negative effect on an IJV's longevity. SMEs' host country knowledge accumulation contributes to a negative relationship between the use of local partners and IJV longevity. Partner bargaining power is a contributing factor to IJV instability. One way to reduce this instability is for the partners to contribute a diverse and continuing set of resources and knowledge, rather than the one-time contribution of host country knowledge, to their international joint ventures. In this way, the dependency between partners is enhanced, the partner bargaining power is less likely to change dramatically, and the IJVs will become more stable.

Given the dependency of the small and medium enterprises on their larger partners' size-based resources, larger firms are in a position to leverage their strong bargaining position and exploit the small and medium enterprises and their international joint ventures.

Is there any way of reducing the likelihood of exploitation?

As discussed, one way to reduce larger partners' incentives of exploitation is to increase the large firm's equity ownership in the IJV. The positive effect of large partners on the longevity of SMEs' IJVs indicates the importance of access to resources and the endorsement effect gained from partnering with large partners. More importantly, it shows that the more difficult it is to replicate the partners' resources, the more stable the IJVs. Compared to host country knowledge, which is an experience-based resource, size-based resources such as financial resources and reputation take a much longer time to develop. SMEs can acquire much more easily their partners' host country knowledge than their size-related resources. Therefore, the contribution of size-related resources leads to IJV longevity while the contribution of host country knowledge increases the exit rates of IJVs.

So if I understand this correctly, there are differing effects that the same strategy could have on different dimensions of firm performance.

That's right.

Let me see if I can summarize this for when I meet with my neighbour next. I have three main conclusions about SMEs and international joint ventures.

One, host country knowledge from local partners is more effective than that from home country partners to improvements in IJV profitability. The local partner presents a primary source of local knowledge, and small and medium enterprises should explore opportunities to seek partnership with local firms in their internationalization in order to benefit from immediate local access associated with such a partnering strategy.

Two, large firms can play an important role in the alleviation of the liabilities of newness and smallness faced by SMEs' international joint ventures. Partnering with large partners can be a viable strategy for SMEs' international joint ventures in the pursuit of longevity. However, small and medium enterprises should be aware of the higher bargaining power of large firms and the possible negative implications of this strategy for IJV profitability when seeking alliances with large firms in their international expansion.

Three, the contrasting effects that host country knowledge and size-based resources had on IJV longevity point to the importance of considering the characteristics of resources contributed by IJV partners. To promote IJV longevity, SMEs could contribute a diverse and continuing set of resources so that there is an ongoing incentive to remain in the joint venture.

That's it.

18

Licensing As a Non-Equity Alliance

You *mentioned earlier that licensing is an example of a non-equity strategic alliance. Can you expand on that?*

Sure. Licensing is a contractual arrangement where the licensor (that's the selling firm) allows its technology, patents, trademarks, designs, processes, know-how, intellectual property, or other proprietary advantages to be used for a fee by the licensee (buying firm). Licensing is a strategy for technology transfer. It is also an approach to internationalization that requires less time or depth of involvement in foreign markets, compared with export strategies, equity joint ventures, and foreign direct investment (FDI).

Most international licensing agreements are between firms from industrialized countries. As well, licensing occurs most frequently in technology-intensive industries. It is not surprising, then, that the overall use of licensing varies a lot from country to country.

A great deal of international licensing also occurs in industries that are not technology-intensive. These industries range from food to sports teams to publishing. Retail sales of licensed merchandise exceeds $100 billion annually. As you know, the popular press is replete with announcements regarding international licensing.

So, when is licensing employed?

Before I answer that, I should point out that many of my comments assume a technology transfer. This would generally constitute a more complex form of licensing than those involving trademarks, for example.

The strategic advantages to be gained by licensing depend on the technology, firm size, product maturity, and extent of the firm's experience. A number of internal and external circumstances may lead a firm to employ a licensing strategy. From the perspective of the licensor, these would vary when:

1. A firm lacks the capital, managerial resources, or knowledge of foreign markets required for exporting or FDI, but it wants to earn additional profits with minimal commitment.
2. You want a way of testing and proactively developing a market that can later be exploited by direct investment.
3. The technology involved is not central to the licensor's core business. Not surprisingly, single—or dominant—product firms are very reluctant to license their core technology, whereas diversified firms are much more willing to license peripheral technologies.
4. Prospects of "technology feedback" are high (i.e., the licensor has been contractually ensured of access to new developments generated by the licensee and based on licensed knowledge).
5. The licensor wishes to exploit its technology in secondary markets that may be too small to justify larger investments; the required economies of scale may not be attainable.
6. Host-country governments restrict imports or FDI, or both; or the risk of nationalization or foreign control is too great.
7. The licensee is unlikely to become a future competitor.
8. The pace of technological change is sufficiently rapid that the licensor can remain technologically superior and ahead of the licensee, who is a potential competitor. As well, if the technology may become obsolete quickly, there is pressure to exploit it fully while the opportunity exists.

From the perspective of the licensee, the main advantage of licensing is that the licensee's existing products or technology can be acquired more cheaply, faster, and with less risk from third parties (licensors) than by internal R&D. Another advantage is that the licensee can gain product designs for a desired diversification, to complement other assets it possesses such as production or marketing capability.

Sounds great, but are there risks associated with licensing?

Yes. The most important risk is the possible loss of one's proprietary advantage, since the licensee acquires at least a portion of the advantage via licensing. Thus, any licensor should try to ensure that its licensee would not be a future competitor or act opportunistically. Not surprisingly, many license agreements are made between firms from different countries so as to reduce the likelihood of creating a competitor in the domestic market. Other approaches include limiting the licensee's market and insisting on technology feedback or flowback clauses.

Licensed trademarks remain the licensor's property in perpetuity, whereas licenses normally have a finite lifetime. A licensor may retain considerable bargaining power in proportion to the perishability of the licensed technology and the licensor's ability to provide a continuing supply of new technology in the future.

A second risk with licensing is that the licensor jeopardizes its worldwide reputation if the licensee cannot maintain the desired product standards and quality or if it engages in questionable practices. Because the licensor will typically become aware of licensee questionable practices only after the fact, this suggests the need to devote more time during the original negotiations to understanding the character of the licensee.

Another consideration with licensing is that profits to the licensor may not be maximized. This is because (a) their involvement in the licensed markets is indirect, (b) exchange rates change, (c) some countries limit the amount of outward payments for licenses, and so forth.

Some of the standard elements of a license agreement are more difficult than others for the licensor to enforce. These would include (a) guaranteeing flowback of actual improvements, (b) sublicensing, (c) diligence that the terms are being honored, and (d) quality control. As a result, sometimes licensing may not provide even the minimum expected benefits.

Peter, you've mentioned a few times the importance of protecting intellectual property rights. Don't our patents protect us?

In many countries intellectual property legislation either does not exist or, more likely, is not enforced. Not surprisingly, a major issue for many companies is infringement of their intellectual property rights. With billions of dollars at stake, this issue has also become a key element in trade negotiations.

Some companies have deemed it necessary to enter into license agreements as a means of offsetting trademark piracy. The logic behind such "reluctant licensing" is that by licensing a local firm the local firm will, in turn, take the necessary steps to stop unlicensed domestic competitors from using the intellectual property.

There are numerous implications with such a scenario. For example, many organizations are feeling pressure to internationalize their operations sooner than they were expecting. As a consequence, they view licensing as a defensive solution, rather than an opportunity.

This has been useful, but it sounds like if you can somehow control the risks, the costs of licensing are pretty low. Right?

Licensing is sometimes incorrectly viewed as a one-time transaction involving little in the way of costs for the licensor. In reality, there are costs associated with (a) the protection of industrial property, (b) establishing the license agreement, and (c) maintaining the license agreement.

Protection costs are not solely the costs of registering one's patents or trademark. They also potentially entail defending one's intellectual property in a court of law.

Establishment costs would include expenses for searching for suitable licensees, communication, training, equipment testing, and so forth. Some products/technologies lend themselves to licensing, while others do not. The greater the cost and complexity of modifying the underlying intellectual property, the more difficult it is to effectively employ a licensing strategy.

Maintenance costs might include backup services for licensees, audit, ongoing market research, and so forth. These are nontrivial expenses. For example, Seattle-based consultants from Starbucks Coffee visit each foreign store (licensee) at least once a month. Monitoring costs will directly and significantly affect the willingness of companies to license or franchise internationally.

To all of these out-of-pocket expenses must be added opportunity costs. Opportunity costs are made up of the loss of current or prospective revenues from exports or other sources.

I knew there had to be a catch. Does any of this vary according to where you license? Are there unattractive markets for licensing?

A number of conditions directly impact "real" licensing returns and make a particular country an unattractive market for licensing. The first of these conditions occurs where there is a regulatory scheme governing licensing. In some countries—such as France, Ireland, and Spain—licenses are not valid until government approval or registration is completed.

Licensing As a Non-Equity Alliance ▪ **133**

A second condition occurs when licenses granting exclusive rights to certain products or territories are not allowed. In some cases, governments may prohibit them because competition will be substantially lessened. Also, some countries place limits on the allowable duration of agreements.

Another condition occurs when there are foreign exchange controls or other restrictions on royalty payments (license fees). Frequently, a withholding tax on royalty payments to nonresident licensors may be applied. In Europe, the combined withholding tax and VAT (value-added tax) can range up to about 50%.

Finally, some countries impose royalty and fee limits. Some use a 10% limit, while others employ a more stringent 3% limit. Any of these government-set rates can, and frequently do, change over time.

Overall, licensing tends to be more attractive when agreements formed in the country enjoy the benefit of freedom of contract. Here the parties may, for the most part, create their own legal framework by the manner in which the contract is written.

How complicated are actual license agreements? What are the major elements of a license agreement?

David, this is a bit of a long list, because the license agreement is the essential commercial contract between licensee and licensor, which specifies the rights to be granted, the consideration payable, and the duration of the terms. The licensed rights usually take the form of patents, registered trademarks, registered industrial designs, unpatented technology, trade secrets, know-how, or copyrights. The license agreement should make explicit reference to the product as well as to the underlying "intangible" or "intellectual" property rights.

Although no definitive standard form exists for license agreements, certain points are typically covered. In many cases, licensors will have developed standard forms for these contracts, based on their past experiences in licensing. Typically, a license agreement will include the following:

1. A clear and correct description of the parties to the agreement, identifying the corporate names of each party, its incorporating jurisdiction, and its principal place of business.
2. A preamble or recitals describing the parties, their reasons for entering into the arrangement, and their respective roles.
3. A list of defined terms for the purposes of the particular contract to simplify this complex document and to eliminate ambiguity or vagueness (e.g., definitions of the terms licensed, product, net profit, territory, and so forth).

4. A set of schedules, in an exhibit or appendix, where necessary, to segregate lengthy detailed descriptions of any kind.
5. The grant that is fundamental to the agreement and explicitly describes the nature of the rights being granted to the licensee. This grant may be based on promotion methods, trade secrets, list of customers, drawings and photographs, models, tools, and parts; or know-how. Know-how, in turn, may be based on invention records, laboratory records, research reports, development reports, engineering reports, pilot plant design, production plant design, production specifications, raw material specifications, quality controls, economic surveys, market surveys, etc.
6. A description of any geographical limitations to be imposed on the licensee's manufacturing, selling, or sublicensing activities.
7. A description of any exclusive rights to manufacture and sell that may be granted.

Wow, this is a long list.

I'm not finished yet David.

8. A discussion of any rights to sublicense.
9. The terms relating to the duration of the agreement, including the initial term and any necessary provisions for the automatic extension or review of the agreement.
10. Provisions for the granting of rights to downstream refinements or improvements made by the licensor in the future.
11. Provisions for "technological flowback" agreements where some benefit of improvements made by the licensee reverts to the licensor. The rights to the future improvements by either the licensor or licensee are often used as leverage in negotiations.
12. Details regarding the royalties or periodic payments based on the use of licensed rights. The percentage rate of the royalty may be fixed or variable (based on time, production level, sales level, and so forth), but the "royalty base" for this rate must be explicitly defined.

So how do you calculate royalties, and is there a best way?

Some of the methods of calculating royalties include percentage of sales, royalties based on production, percentage of net profit, lump-sum payments, or payment-free licenses in cross-licensing arrangements.

There are no hard-and-fast rules for establishing royalty rates. One arbitrary rule suggests that the licensor aim for a 25% share of the licensee's related profits and then convert this profit level to a certain royalty rate. Others suggest that licensors will often specify a minimum or target absolute compensation. This can be derived from technology transfer cost considerations or a judgment of how much it may cost the prospective licensee to acquire the technology by other means or from an "industry norm." Royalty escalation clauses and the currency of payment should also be specified.

It is often quite difficult for the licensor to accurately estimate the market potential for its property. As a consequence, the licensee, with its greater knowledge of local conditions, is often in a stronger position when the royalty rate terms are being negotiated.

Wow, this sure is a long list.

Almost done David.

13. Specification of minimum performance requirements (e.g., minimum royalty payments, unit sales volumes, employment of personnel, minimum promotion expenditures, and so forth) to ensure the "best efforts" of the licensee so that the license potential is fully exploited. For example, most license agreements that confer exclusive selling rights in a given area to the licensee also require either a sizable down payment or a minimum annual royalty payment. Otherwise, the licensee may "sit on" the license and block the licensor from entering the market in question.
14. Other clauses common to most license agreements include those to protect the licensed rights against licensees and third parties and those regarding title retention by the licensor, confidentiality of know-how, quality control, most-favored-licensee status, the applicable language of the contract, and any provisions with respect to the assignability of rights by the licensee.

The above list of elements common to most license agreements is by no means exhaustive. Every license agreement is unique in some way and, therefore, great care should be taken in its negotiation and formal documentation.

Peter: Excuse me but I need to get a little shuteye.

Postscript

Even though our flight has landed Peter, I'd still like to get your views on a few more questions I have. Can I give you a ride to your hotel? In fact, where are you staying? Maybe I should change hotels.

Thanks for the offer, David, but there will be a driver who will be picking me up, and for the next few days I'm going to be fully occupied with the joint venture facilitation I came here for. Then I'm going straight away to Singapore.

Can I call you if I've got questions?

David: Everyone involved with joint ventures will have questions. And no one, least of all me, will have all the answers. I encourage you to think about the principles we've discussed. They work.

In addition, here's a reading list (see Appendix) of case studies that deal with joint ventures.

What about after my joint venture is operational? I can imagine that I'll have lots of new questions then.

I'm sure you will. But I'm sure you'll be up for the challenge.

How can I reach you?

Here, let me give you a business card.

Thanks. Whoa! This card is in Chinese or something.

Just turn it over. Look at it from the other side. It will be clearer then.

Maybe in a few years time I'll see you again on this flight. Then we can discuss my next set of questions.

I'll rest up.

Chapter End Notes

Chapter 1

The source of the "model husbands club" story was Professor Tamer Cavusgil of Michigan State University. He shared it at a conference at The University of South Carolina in 1992.

There are a number of international strategy texts readily available. See, for example, Bartlett, Ghoshal and Beamish (2008) or Beamish, Morrison, Inkpen, and Rosenzweig (2003).

Chapter 2

One of the world's leading centers for research on international joint ventures and alliances is the Ivey Business School at the University of Western Ontario. It's faculty, PhD program graduates (and candidates) have already (co)authored over 150 publications as at January 2008: 110 articles, 10 books and 38 contributed chapters. Their efforts are on going. To download abstracts of any of the JV articles, go to http://www.ivey.uwo.ca/ami/Research/JVA.htm. There is no charge.

For access to the abstracts of the Ivey research to date resulting from the massive database on Japanese foreign direct investment, go to http://www.ivey.uwo.ca/ami/Research/JFDI.htm. Note: not all of this body of research relates to joint ventures.

For more detail on the IKEA and Kentucky Fried Chicken in China case studies, go to Ivey Publishing [http://www.ivey.uwo.ca/cases] to order copies. There is a modest charge. The full case names and numbers are: IKEA (Canada) Ltd. 1986 (Condensed) [9A88M010], Kentucky Fried Chicken in China (A) [9A90G001]; Kentucky Fried Chicken in China (B) [9A90G002], and Kentucky Fried Chicken in China (C) [9A90G003].

For those seeking more information on other forms of alliances, see for example Doz and Hamel (1998), Gomes-Casseres (1996), Contractor and Lorange (1988), and the four-part series "Strategic Alliances That Work" [9B05M022–9B05M025] by Jean-Louis Schaan and Micheal Kelly available through Ivey Publishing.

For more detail on JV profitability, see Delios and Beamish (2004).

Chapter 3

To order a copy of the Atlas of Global Development, go to [http://www.worldbank.org/] or HarperCollins Publishers.

On the next page is the completed Ranking Table and below are a few observations on these important demographic statistics.

Population

- There are two billion-person-plus countries.
- Nearly all of the most populous countries are in the developing world.
- Most people are unaware of how populous the following countries are: Indonesia, Pakistan, and Bangladesh.
- The populations of several of the most populous countries are flat/declining: Russia, Japan.
- Only one country in Western Europe makes the top 12 list: Germany.
- The population of the Indian subcontinent exceeds that of China.

GNI

- 7 of the 9 largest economies are the original G7 (the exceptions are China and Spain).
- Half of the top 12 countries by economic size were not on the top 12 countries by population list (UK, France, Italy, Canada, Spain, S. Korea).
- Similarly half of the top 12 countries by population drop off the list of the top 12 economies by output (Indonesia, Brazil, Pakistan, Russia, Bangladesh, Nigeria).

Top Twelve Rankings

Rank	Purchasing Power Parity GDP[a] (Int'l $ Billion) Economic output measured by looking at the prices of a bundle of goods and services at home in local currencies		Gross National Income[b] (GNI) (in U.S. $ Billion) Economic output measured by valuing each country's goods and services in dollars, using three year average exchange rates		Population[b] (Million)	
1	United States	12,970	United States	12,970	China	1,305
2	China	10,000	Japan	4,988	India	1,095
3	Japan	4,220	Germany	2,852	United States	297
4	India	4,042	China	2,264	Indonesia	220
5	Germany	2,585	United Kingdom	2,263	Brazil	186
6	United Kingdom	1,903	France	2,178	Pakistan	156
7	France	1,871	Italy	1,724	Russia	143
8	Italy	1,727	Spain	1,100	Bangladesh	142
9	Russia	1,723	Canada	1,052	Nigeria	132
10	Brazil	1,616	India	793	Japan	128
11	South Korea	1,180	S. Korea	765	Mexico	103
12	Canada	1,165	Mexico	753	Germany	83

[a] Source: *The World Fact Book* as of March 15/07; most are estimates for 2006.
[b] Source: *2007 Atlas of Global Development*, figures for 2005.

PPP

- The USA is used as the base case, so its level is the same whether in terms of GNI or PPP.
- China moves from #4 using GNI to #2 worldwide using PPP.
- In most countries, the PPP rate exceeds the GNI rate: a major exception is Japan.
- Two of the three largest economies are in Asia-Pacific.

For more on the role of one's international mindset, and its link to performance, see Calof and Beamish (1994). Based on a typology developed by Wharton's Howard Perlmutter, they argue that everyone has a centric profile, or dominant attitude, toward foreign cultures. The basic attitude types are ethnocentric (stick with what we do at home because it will be superior to the practices elsewhere), polycentric (use local practices: 'When in Rome, do as the Romans do'), and geocentric (selectively draw from the best of home country and foreign practices). They found that firms with senior managers who held geocentric mindsets had far higher international sales.

Chapter 4

Some of the Examples in this chapter are drawn from Beamish (2003) that in turn are drawn from earlier editions of the textbook chapter originally prepared by Peter Killing.

Chapter 6

The graphic on effect of equity on mortality risk in this chapter is from Dhanaraj and Beamish (2004) and is used with permission of the publisher (*Strategic Management Journal*).

The graphic about the interaction effect between subsidiary age and cultural distance on ownership level is from Wilkinson, Peng, Brouthers and Beamish (2008) and is used with permission of the publisher (*Journal of International Management*).

Chapter 7

Much of the material in this chapter is taken directly from Lane and Beamish (1990) and is used with permission of the publisher (*Management International Review*). For this and some of the other chapters, go to the original source for a more complete treatment of the issue. The original journal articles will contain the theoretical bases for the argument, data sources, and full academic references.

Chapter 8

Some of the portion of this chapter, which deals with organizational climate similarity, is taken directly from Fey and Beamish (2001) and is used with permission of the publisher (*Organization Studies*).

Chapter 9

For more on the principal elements of a Joint Venture Agreement, see for example "Teaming Up for the Nineties—Can You Survive Without a Partner?" Source: Deloitte, Haskins and Sells International (undated), or Reiter and Shishler (1999).

Some of the material in the latter part of this chapter that relates to Making the Joint Venture Work is from Beamish (2003) and is used with the permission of the publisher (*McGraw-Hill*).

Chapter 10

For early perspectives on joint ventures in a developed country context, see Killing (1983) and Harrigan (1985).

Portions of this chapter are drawn from Choi and Beamish (2004) and are used with the permission of the publisher (*Journal of International Business Studies*).

For much more detail on the examples of dominant control, shared control and split control joint ventures, see the full Ivey cases: "Sun Life Financial: Entering China" [9B04M066] by Paul Beamish, Ken Mark and Jordan Mitchell; "Bundy Asia Pacific—China Strategy" [9A98M003] by

Paul Beamish, Jack Li, Nancy Wang and Steven Zuo; and "Toppan Moore" [9A92G001] by Paul Beamish and Shige Makino.

Chapter 11

The example used in this chapter is derived from the Ivey case "Nora-Sakari: A Proposed Joint Venture in Malaysia" [9A95G002] by Paul Beamish and Azimah Ainuddin.

On occasion, one still hears some people talking about how they squeezed a great deal out of their JV partner. This is not the right approach in a JV negotiation. When my youngest son was 14 years old, we took a family trip to South Asia that included a week in Bali. He prepared the guidelines below for negotiating with street vendors. A street vendor is not a potential joint venture partner, and should not be treated like one.

1. If you want a bicycle, start by asking for a car.
2. *Every* price that they give is a special price, don't feel lucky.
3. Unless there is war, famine or catastrophe, they won't sell for a loss.
4. Be prepared to walk away and come back later.
5. Do not carry large sums of money with you and do not show the merchant all your money.
6. If they reach the price you name you must buy it; do not try to then go any lower. Don't engage in negotiation unless you intend to buy.
7. If you're just browsing, tell them.
8. The first price is *never* the final price.
9. Never say that you *like* the product.

Chapter 12

Much of this chapter including the list of strategies for dealing with JV conflict is drawn from Fey and Beamish (1999); and is used with the permission of the publisher (*European Management Journal*).

Chapter 13

Some of the material from this chapter is taken from Beamish and Berdrow (2003) and is used with the permission of the publisher (*Long Range Planning*).

The reasons why parent firms do not harvest knowledge from IJVs are from Inkpen and Crossan (1995).

An example of an Ivey case in which learning opportunities are identified by a JV general manager, but not valued by one of the partners, would be "Wil-Mor Technologies" [9A99M042] by Andrew Inkpen. This case examines a US-Japanese JV in the auto parts sector.

The descriptions about the Office of Alliance Management at Lilly are taken directly from the Ivey case study by Dhanaraj, Lyles and Lui, "Innovation Without Walls: Alliance Management at Eli Lilly and Company" [9B07M015].

Chapter 14

This chapter draws heavily on the award winning dissertation by Chris Changwha Chung which was completed in June 2006, "The Evolution of International Joint Ventures: Multiple Waves of Structural Change."

Chapter 15

The key arguments in this chapter are taken from Makino et al. (2007). It is used with the permission of the publisher (*Strategic Management Journal*).

Chapter 16

Most of the arguments in this chapter are drawn from Beamish and Kachra (2004). It is used with the permission of the publisher (*Journal of World Business*).

Chapter 17

Much of the material from this chapter is taken from Lu and Beamish (2006) and is used with the permission of the publisher (*Journal of Business Venturing*). This and other chapters were supplemented with material from Beamish (1999) that is used with the permission of the publisher (*JAI Press*).

The origins of the four liabilities relate respectively to work by Stinchcombe (1965) re: liability of newness, Hannan and Freeman (1989) re: liability of size, Hymer (1960) re: liability of foreignness, and Beamish (1999) re: liability of relational orientation.

Chapter 18

A closely related contractual arrangement to licensing is franchising. Franchising is an organizational form where the franchisor (parent company/owner) of a service, trademarked product, or brand name allows the franchisee to use the same in return for a lump sum payment and/or royalty, while conforming to required standards of quality, service, and so forth.

From a global perspective, nearly 800 franchisors have sold franchises abroad, accounting for tens of thousands of overseas locations. For example, over half of KFC's more than 11,000 locations are outside the USA, and of these, the majority is via franchise.

For a more detailed discussion of licensing, see the Note on International Licensing registered with Ivey Publishing (product # 9B06M005). It contains supplementary reading lists, examples of international licensing announcements, and a detailed (9-page) checklist for license agreements.

Appendix: Case Abstracts

Cases Referenced in End Notes

IKEA (Canada) Ltd.—1986 (Condensed) [9A88M010]
by Paul W. Beamish

The mid-1986 Sears new catalogue contained a 20-page section called Elements. This section bore a striking resemblance to the format of an IKEA catalogue, and the furniture being offered was similar to IKEA'S knocked-down self-assembly line. The head of IKEA'S North American operations wondered how serious Sears was about its new initiative and what, if anything, IKEA should do in response.

Kentucky Fried Chicken in China (A) [9A90G001]
by Allen Morrison, Paul W. Beamish

The new vice-president for Kentucky Fried Chicken in Southeast Asia must weigh the growth benefits of investing in China with alternative opportunities in the region. He is at the exploratory stage of market research and is focusing his attention on four possible locations in China. He must also balance his own personal ambitions with the possibilities for failure, not only in China, but the rest of Southeast Asia.

Kentucky Fried Chicken in China (B) [9A90G002]

by Allen Morrison, Paul W. Beamish

The VP's efforts to determine whether and how to proceed with an emerging three-way partnership in China are described. Kentucky Fried Chicken has selected local partners and has been issued a license to operate a restaurant in Beijing. If he is to proceed, the VP must decide how fast he should advance the negotiations and which of three location sites in the city is most desirable.

Kentucky Fried Chicken in China (C) [9A90G003]

by Allen Morrison, Paul W. Beamish

This case presents the start-up of operations in Beijing and discusses the difficulties Kentucky Fried Chicken (KFC) is having with its local partners. By March 1988, KFC has established its largest restaurant in the world in Beijing with sales that are booming and showing no sign of slowing down. Nevertheless, the extent of operational problems and the shortage of hard currency profits are raising concerns over whether further expansion is warranted.

Strategic Alliances That Work: Implementing Winning Conditions [9B05M025]

by Micheal Kelly, Jean-Louis Schaan

This note is part of a series entitled Strategic Alliances That Work. All the strategic analysis, negotiation, and implementation planning of a strategic alliance aims for the day the alliance can be formally launched. While many of the details depend on the specific nature of the agreement, there exist common practices that will take you far down the path of successful alliance management. These include laying a positive foundation with the right team and establishing productive linkages across both organizations. It also includes dedicated focus on building trusted relationships in the early days and structuring alliance activities for some early successes. Alliances usually define success in terms of financial returns; but when the honeymoon is over, enduring and sustainable benefits will be more easily achieved through additional emphasis on effective communications, constructive conflict resolution and continuous organizational learning—elements that support a productive relationship over time.

Strategic Alliances That Work: Negotiating and Designing an Alliance [9B05M024]

by Micheal Kelly, Jean-Louis Schaan

The negotiation process involves pre-negotiation preparations such as putting together the negotiating team, conducting the negotiation itself, and finalizing the ultimate agreement. The agreement should address, among other things, the mission of the alliance, its structure and governance, ownership and control details, identification of performance objectives and milestones, conflict resolution procedures, and provision for termination of the partnership.

Strategic Alliances That Work: Selecting the Right Partner [9B05M023]

by Micheal Kelly, Jean-Louis Schaan

Key factors to consider during the selection process are the overall strategic fit between potential partners, the complementarities of each organization's strengths, weaknesses and operational practices, the sustainability of the relationship, consideration of how partner cultures may clash or complement one another, the degree of commitment to the partnership, and finally, the personal chemistry between both companies' management.

Strategic Alliances That Work: Should You Build a Strategic Alliance [9B05M022]

by Micheal Kelly, Jean-Louis Schaan

This note provides guidelines to determine whether an alliance is an appropriate vehicle to pursue business objectives. Specifically, it covers areas such as the strategic rationale for the alliance, the identification of competence and resource gaps in relation to strategic objectives, and a firm's readiness to enter a collaborative arrangement.

Sun Life Financial: Entering China [9B04M066]

by Paul W. Beamish, Ken Mark, Jordan Mitchell

Sun Life Financial is a large insurance conglomerate with $14.7 billion in annual revenues. The vice-president for China must formulate an approach for his company's entrance into China. Sun Life has achieved two important milestones: the right to apply for license and the signing of a

Memorandum of Understanding for Joint Venture with China Everbright, a local securities company. The financial vice-president must consider strategic options for entry and choose a city in which to focus his efforts in getting a license. In doing so, he needs to consider Sun Life's overall priorities, strategic direction and how he will sell the concept to senior management in Canada. Intended for use in an introduction to international business course, the case includes assessing internal capabilities against an environmental scan, formulating strategy and making operational decisions relating to city selection. It also introduces the idea of joint venture management and government relations.

Bundy Asia Pacific—China Strategy [9A98M003]

by Paul W. Beamish, Jack Li, Nancy Wang, Steven Zuo

Phil Stephenson, the director of China for Bundy Asia Pacific (BAP), was preoccupied with Bundy's business in China. BAP's CEO, Tony Martin, had shown Phil the fax from Robin Thompson, the new marketing and product development director of Bundy International, BAP's UK-based parent company. Thompson had asked BAP about its strategy for the refrigeration business in China. Despite 10 years of experience in China, Bundy had not met its market goals. Whatever strategy was developed, it would be an important part of Bundy's proposed global refrigeration strategy. This rich case allows detailed discussion around issues including (a) business (re)development strategy, (b) joint ventures versus wholly owned subsidiaries, (c) organizational structure, and (d) expatriate and local staffing.

Toppan Moore [9A92G001]

by Paul W. Beamish, Shigefumi Makino, Joyce Miller

The semi-annual meeting of the board of Toppan Moore, a joint venture between Toppan Printing of Japan and Moore Corporation of Canada, took place in Tokyo. With sales exceeding US$1 billion, Toppan Moore was a leader in the Japanese business forms industry and widely considered one of the most successful international joint ventures in Japan. While pleased with the venture's recent results, the issue for the board members was how to ensure continued prosperity.

Nora-Sakari: A Proposed JV in Malaysia (Revised) [9B06M006]

by Paul W. Beamish, R. Azimah Ainuddin

This case presents the perspective of a Malaysian company, Nora Bhd, which was in the process of trying to establish a telecommunications joint venture with a Finnish firm, Sakari Oy. Negotiations have broken down between the firms, and students are asked to try to restructure a win-win deal. The case examines some of the most common issues involved in partner selection and design in international joint ventures.

Wil-Mor Techologies: Is There a Crisis? [9A99M042]

by Andrew C. Inkpen

The CEO of Wilson Industries, a U.S. firm, is concerned about the performance of a joint venture between Wilson Industries and a Japanese firm, Morota Manufacturing. He wants the joint venture president to make some changes to improve financial performance. However, the president is unsure of what action to take because the Japanese partner, Morota, is satisfied with the performance and is considering expansion plans.

Innovation Without Walls: Alliance Management at Eli Lilly and Company [9B07M015]

by Charles Dhanaraj, Marjorie Lyles, YuPeng Lai

The newly appointed executive director of the Office of Alliance Management (OAM) at Eli Lilly and Company (Lilly) was returning to his office after his first meeting with his supervisor, the senior vice-president of Corporate Strategy and Business Development (CSBD). The executive director had been promoted to the position just a week earlier, and now the senior vice-president has asked him to conduct a complete review of the OAM strategy. The senior vice-president made it clear that it was fine to leave the strategy as it currently existed, or to change it radically if the situation warranted. Now the executive director must decide what Lilly should do to build and maintain its leadership in alliance capability.

Note on International Licensing [9B06M005]

by Paul W. Beamish

Licensing is a strategy for technology transfer; and an approach to internationalization that requires less time or depth of involvement in foreign markets, compared to exports, joint ventures, and foreign direct investment. This note examines when licensing is employed, risks associated with it, intellectual property rights, costs of licensing, unattractive markets for licensing, and the major elements of the license agreement.

Additional Joint Venture Cases (All Available from Ivey Publishing)

Eagle Services Asia [9B07D019]

by Edward D. Arnheiter

This case study chronicles the creation and transformation of a Singaporean joint venture, Eagle Services Asia (ESA). The case describes some early start-up problems, including a forced shutdown by the Civilian Aviation Authority of Singapore (CAAS). The resulting shakeup of the ESA management team provides a fresh start and an opportunity to reinvigorate the company using lean management principles. Managerial decisions play a key role in ESA's success, together with the discipline and training of the workforce. Students will gain an understanding of cultural difficulties associated with international joint ventures, and learn fundamental aspects of lean management including how to create and sustain a lean culture. The case also provides insight into the worldwide aircraft engine business, the engine overhaul process and cultural barriers that may arise when managing operations in foreign countries.

Mahindra & Mahindra Ltd.—Farm Equipment Sector: Acquisition of Jiangling Tractor Company [9B07M035]

by Jean-Louis Schaan, Ramasastry Chandrasekhar

Farm Equipment Services (FES), the tractor manufacturing division of Mahindra & Mahindra Ltd. (M&M), is considering entering the Chinese tractor industry through a joint venture with Jiangling Tractor Company (JTC), a state-owned automotive enterprise. M&M had seeded the Chinese tractor market with exports and had concluded that the most efficient and prudent way to serve the Chinese tractor market was through a joint venture with a local partner. JTC had good brand recognition and strong position in the small tractor market. However, due to the lack of interest from the parent company, Jiangling Motor Company Group, JTC was facing severe operational challenges: was over staffed, had high overhead, owed significant amounts to suppliers and dealers were fleeing the company. M&M saw an opportunity to work with a management team they were comfortable with and to leverage JTC's potential to grow in China and to export tractors as well as components. The challenge was to determine how management should proceed to restructure and integrate the joint ventures assets.

Orchid Chemicals & Pharmaceuticals Limited: Managing the Value Chain Transformation [9B06M071]

by Ravi N. Ravichandran, Ankur Roy

Orchid Chemicals & Pharmaceuticals Limited (Orchid) is an Indian pharmaceutical company, which commenced its operations in 1994. Over a span of 10 years, the turnover of this company has increased from US$11 million to US$153 million. The company's profit after tax registered a fivefold increase from US$1.3 million to US$6.8 million in the corresponding period. Early success was a combination of pricing flexibility, lower production cost and business opportunities in unregulated markets. Orchid decided to explore opportunities for the manufacture of generic drugs in the regulated markets and formulations in the domestic market. Diversification to basic research was also considered. Cooperation and joint ventures were the primary route to expand and explore new molecule discovery. By 2005, Orchid was no longer a single-product company, its business had widened to multiple products in bulk, formulations and generics, in both regulated and unregulated markets. Orchid was making its presence felt in its novel drug delivery systems and new drug development processes. In 2005, Orchid faced several challenges related to financial leverage and risks, leadership, managerial challenges associated with joint ventures, balancing the new business model, setting global trends in being a pioneer in the industry, addressing shareholders' concerns and evolving an appropriate organization culture and process.

Activplant: The European Opportunity [9B06M046]

by Stewart Thornhill

Activplant is a software firm specializing in monitoring, measuring and analyzing the performance of factory automation systems in London, Ontario, Canada. It is a pioneer of the industry, and has installations in most of the largest automobile manufacturing firms in North America as well as some clients in consumer goods. Activplant is considering the opportunity of expanding their business to include a much more aggressive sales and service approach in Europe. An entrance into Europe involves how both sales and service will be delivered to clients, which could be done through a number of different channels including: consulting partners, value-added resellers, a joint venture or fulltime Activplant staff. The case allows students to evaluate both the dollar costs and benefits of each choice as well as qualitative concerns like product quality and maintaining contact with customers.

Velsicol Eesti AS (A): A U.S.-Estonian Joint Venture [9B00M007]

by Iris Berdrow

Velsicol Chemical Corporation, a global company focused on producing specialty chemicals, has formed a joint venture with the Estonian government called Velsicol Eesti AS that would produce benzoic acid. The plant that will produce this chemical was previously part of a conglomerate owned and controlled by the Russian government. When Estonia became an independent state this plant was passed on to the country that then privatized and sold a percentage of it to Velsicol. The newly appointed plant manager came from a benzoic plant outside the country and was responsible for government relations, cost management, liaison with the board of directors, performance standards and staffing. He must quickly put together a management team that would be familiar with the current operations and capable of working together to achieve the company's goals. In order to do this, he needed to better understand the employees with whom he was working.

Resina: Managing Operations in China [9B06M048]

by Paul W. Beamish, Jordan Mitchell

Resina is a global manufacturer of resins and surfacing solutions headquartered in Helsinki, Finland, and has three production facilities and 12 sales offices in China. The head of Asia Pacific for Resina needs to decide what should be done about Beijing and Guangdong. Should Beijing remain in operation, be shut down, or moved to another area where demand for liquid bulk resins is stronger? Similar options exist in Guangdong. In aiming towards profitable operations, he needs to consider the buoyancy of local demand, Resina's partner in Beijing, local and foreign competitors and appropriate managers in each operation.

Alpes S.A.: A Joint Venture Proposal (A) [9B06M027]

by Henry W. Lane, Dennis Shaughnessy, David T. A. Wesley

The senior vice-president for corporate development for Charles River Laboratories must prepare a presentation to the company's board of directors requesting up to a $2 million investment in a Mexican joint venture with a family-owned animal health company. However, the chief executive officer views the proposed joint venture as a potential distraction while his company continues to expand rapidly in the United States. He is also worried about the risks of investing in a country like Mexico and the plan to partner with a small, family-owned company. Moreover, the Mexican partner is unable to invest any cash in the joint venture, which would need to be fully funded by Charles River Laboratories.

Cameron Auto Parts (B)—Revised [9B06M016]
by Harold Crookell, Paul W. Beamish

Two years after signing a license agreement in the U.K., the company now faces an opportunity to establish with another firm a joint venture in France for the European market. However, the prospect upsets the U.K. licensee who is clearly doing very well, and who even wants Cameron to consider joint venturing with him in Australia. The case ends with Cameron, run off its feet in North America, trying to decide whether to enter Europe via licensing, joint venture or direct investment.

Allison Transmission: Creating a European Face [9B04M045]
by Charles Dhanaraj

Allison Transmission Division is a $2 billion unit within General Motors (GM) with a very specialized product—heavy-duty automatic transmissions for commercial vehicles. Although the division is part of GM, more than 90% of its output is directed to external customers. The case presents a familiar challenge faced by many globalizing firms: a pioneer and leader in a market holding more the 60% of the market in North America, but less than 10% outside North America. The presence of leading original equipment manufacturers in Europe who are the key customers for Allison, and the large market potential in Europe presents a strategic opportunity, but the cultural and institutional differences present a formidable challenge. The technological differences in Europe augments this challenge and the uncertainty surrounding a new hybrid technology that is emerging in Europe make the decision even more complex. Also presented are the company's attempts in Europe for a decade leading to the trigger issue—a decision between a joint venture in Austria and a wholly owned unit in Hungary. The case provides a rich organizational context to challenge students to go beyond a typical alternative analysis to consider the broad strategic issues and identify a comprehensive strategy for Europe.

Taming the Dragon: Cummins in China (Condensed) [9B05M034]
by Charles Dhanaraj, Maria Morgan, Jing Li, Paul W. Beamish

This case documents more than 15 years of U.S.-based Cummins, a global leader in diesel and allied technology, and its investment activities in China. While the macro level indicators seem to suggest the possibility to hit $1 billion in revenues in China by 2005, there were several pressing problems that put into question Cummins' ability to realize this target. Students are presented with four specific situations and must develop an appropriate action plan. They are related to the respective streamlining and consolidation of several existing joint ventures, distribution and service, and staffing. The case presents the complexity of managing country level operations and the role of executive leadership of a country manager.

Eli Lilly in India: Rethinking the Joint Venture Strategy [9B04M016]
by Charles Dhanaraj, Paul W. Beamish, Nikhil Celly

Eli Lilly and Company is a leading U.S. pharmaceutical company. The new president of intercontinental operations is re-evaluating all of the company's divisions, including the joint venture with Ranbaxy Laboratories Limited, one of India's largest pharmaceutical companies. This joint venture has run smoothly for a number of years despite their difference in focus, but recently Ranbaxy was experiencing cash flow difficulties due to its network of international sales. In addition, the Indian government was changing regulations for businesses in India, and joining the World Trade Organization would have an effect on India's chemical and drug regulations. The president must determine if this international joint venture still fits Eli Lilly's strategic objectives.

ASIMCO International Casting Company (A) [9B04D009]
by Robert Klassen, Sophia Liu

ASIMCO International Casting Company, a joint venture between ASIMCO and Caterpillar, had recently finished several major projects designed to upgrade the manufacturing capabilities in its foundry. The plant was now under significant pressure to increase revenue, and had received an invitation to bid on a new customer order. While this order might provide the ideal opportunity to further upgrade its process technology and capabilities, significant challenges were presented by several critical product characteristics. Alternatively, the plant's limited resources could focus on meeting the internal needs of one of its partners. Caterpillar was expected to authorize test runs of two new products soon; however, the annual production volumes were very uncertain.

Cambridge Laboratories: Proteomics [9B04M013]
Henry W. Lane, Dennis Shaughnessy, David T. A. Wesley

Cambridge Laboratories is essentially a fee-for-service provider of laboratory tests. It spends less than 0.5% of revenues on research and development and holds relatively few patents for a biotech company. It now has an opportunity to invest $5 million to establish a joint venture with an Australian proteomics company that operates on a drug discovery (royalty) model. The founder of this company believed that his technology could eventually result in the discovery of new drugs that would generate significant royalties. While the proteomics firm has superb technology, some of the intellectual leaders in the field on its staff, and partnerships with some impressive companies, its technology is yet unproven. Cambridge Labs is also concerned that its existing relationships with big pharmaceutical companies could be jeopardized if it begins to take an intellectual property position in proteomics. In addition, the Australian company consists primarily of PhDs in molecular biology, while business executives whose primary focus is generating strong financial returns for shareholders dominate Cambridge Labs. The cultural differences between an Australian science-oriented laboratory and a publicly traded American outsourcing company become apparent during the negotiation phase of the joint venture proposal. Students are asked to evaluate the joint venture and consider whether the cultural and strategic differences can be reconciled.

Larson in Nigeria (Revised) [9B04M012]

by Paul W. Beamish, Isaiah A. Litvak, Harry Cheung

The vice-president of international operations must decide whether to continue to operate or abandon the company's Nigerian joint venture. Although the expatriate general manager of the Nigerian operation has delivered a very pessimistic report, Larson's own hunch was to stay in that country. Maintaining the operation was complicated by problems in staffing, complying with a promise to increase the share of local ownership, a joint venture partner with divergent views, and increasing costs of doing business in Nigeria. If Larson decides to maintain the existing operation, the issues of increasing local equity participation (i.e. coping with indigenization) and staffing problems (especially in terms of the joint venture general manager) have to be addressed.

General Motors Defense [9B03M002]

by Paul W. Beamish, Changwha Chung

General Motors Defense, a division of General Motors, one of the world's largest automobile manufacturers, designs and manufactures light armored vehicles. The company is approached by General Dynamics to jointly pursue the U.S. Army's Brigade Combat Team program. However, General Dynamic made it clear that they would also submit a bid on their own. Contrary to past practices, the chief of staff of the U.S. Army planned to award the multi-billion dollar contract within only 11 months. The executive director of General Motors Defense has to decide whether the company should bid-it-alone or submit a joint venture bid with General Dynamics.

Wuhan Erie Polymers Joint Venture [9B03C002]

by Thomas Begley, Cynthia Lee, Kenneth Law

The Erie Performance Polymers division manager in China and general manager of Wuhan Erie Polymers joint venture, has just received approval for his requested transfer to divisional headquarters in the United States. In preparing the division and joint venture for the change, a key decision concerns his successor. He has received information on six candidates under consideration and knows that his recommendation will carry heavy weight in the final decision. The general manager has attempted to inculcate in his mainly Chinese workforce an appreciation for Western business practices and ability to enact them. At the same time, acknowledging their substantial differences, he has tried to mix elements of both Chinese and Western values in creating a culture for the joint venture. He believes strongly that his successor must be responsive to the tensions between the relevant cultures. As he compares them, he wonders which candidate has the best set of qualities to succeed him as general manager.

AOL Latin America [9B02M029]

by Henry W. Lane, Nicholas Athanassiou, David T. A. Wesley

America Online (AOL) announced a joint venture to develop a Latin American version of its popular online service. The future seemed bright: AOL had enjoyed phenomenal success in the United States, Latin America was one of the fastest growing markets for online services and the president of AOL Brazil was the former country manager for Brazil's leading telecommunications provider. Despite these factors, the company endures many setbacks. The president leaves to join a competitor's firm, hundreds of the company's CD-ROM discs are discovered to be faulty and potential customers are subscribing with its competitors. AOL's experiences provide a basis for discussing difficulties faced by many multinational companies, including the implications of infrastructure differences, strategic human resources management and the local competition.

Terralumen S.A.: The Blue Ridge Decision [9B02M009]

by David T. A. Wesley, Nicholas Athanassiou, Jeanne McNett

Terralumen is a family-owned agricultural company that has expanded into consumer products. A senior executive with the company has helped build a successful joint venture over a period of 16 years with Delta, an American fast food chain. After a directors meeting, he senses that the American joint venture partners want to end the partnership, but he is unsure why. The joint venture has been profitable, and he also believes his company contributed the most to its success and that prior to the joint venture Delta had limited success in foreign markets. With the break up of the joint venture pending, he must determine how to extract the largest return on Terralumen's investment.

Blue Ridge Spain [9B02M003]

by Nicholas Athanassiou, Henry W. Lane, David T. A. Wesley, Jeanne McNett

Blue Ridge Spain was a joint venture established between a well-known American fast food chain and an "old guard" family-run agricultural company that was seeking to diversify in the wake of Spain's entry into the European Union. The European Regional director of the company has been dealt an unexpected professional blow. After several years of fostering a successful joint venture, the regional director is stunned to find out that the new owners of Blue Ridge want out of the arrangement. In spite of the fact that this particular joint venture has been profitable since its inception and the company has experienced brisk growth during that time, the new owners are determined to end the partnership. The regional director is left examining how he is to respond to a request that he feels is not only detrimental to his company, but also contrary to his principles. He questions the ethics of secretly undermining the joint venture in order to achieve the upper hand in buyout negotiations. As a Greek, the importance of personal relationships and social contracts only adds to his dilemma.

Textron Ltd. [9B01M070]

by Lawrence Beer

Textron Ltd. is a family-owned manufacturer of cotton and sponge fabricated items. The company wants to expand its business with an offshore manufacturing enterprise that will fit with the company's policy of caring for their employees and providing quality products. The company is looking at two options: a guaranteed outsourcing purchase agreement or a joint venture. After several meetings with offshore alliance candidates the vice-president of the company must analyze the cross-cultural differences to established corporate guidelines of global ethics and social responsibility that the company can use in their negotiations with a foreign manufacturing firm.

Welcome Pharmaceuticals [9B01B028]
by David J. Sharp, Alan (Wenchu) Yang

Welcome Pharmaceuticals was a joint venture between North China Pharmaceutical Corp. and Hong Kong Triple Well International and is a leading producer of vitamin C in China. The company's general manager had just returned from an industry wide meeting, and was disturbed by what he had learned: there was a worldwide oversupply of vitamin C and already sagging prices had not yet hit rock bottom. The general manager knew the only way for Welcome to survive was to reduce costs, and because Welcome's material costs were already among the lowest in the industry, the only area left to trim was labor costs. The management team was called together to decide whether this was, in fact, the company's only option. If so, the management team had to quickly decide how to go about affecting what was bound to be an unpopular change among several tiers of workers.

Beijing Jeep Co. and the WTO [9B01M061]
by Justin Tan, Michael N. Young

Beijing Jeep Corporation Ltd. was one of the first joint ventures between an American company, DaimlerChrysler Corporation and a Chinese enterprise, Beijing Automotive Works. Early in its operations, Beijing Jeep was given preferential treatment on tariffs and foreign exchange, and had spent many years developing relationships with senior government officials that protected them from import competition. After several years of negotiations, there was an agreement of terms for China to enter into the World Trade Organization. Terms of this agreement called for a steep reduction in tariffs for imported automobiles, which would lower entry barriers to the Chinese automotive industry, thus creating more competition for the company. Tariffs on components imported from the United States would also be reduced but this would not be enough to offset the flood of imported vehicles into the market. Entry into the World Trade Organization would mean a lot of changes, and Beijing Jeep must determine whether they should continue focusing on the relationships they have built with the government, or approach their joint venture partner for additional support.

Canadian Closures (A) [9B00M019]

by Louis Hebert, Davin Li

Canadian Closures was a joint venture (JV) between the Australian firm, Melbourne Closures (Melbourne), and Macklin Breweries (Macklin) that was based in Canada. The JV manufactured beer bottle caps based on Melbourne's technology; its only customer was Macklin's 10 breweries. Continuing product quality and performance problems resulted in the general manager being replaced. The new general manager was faced with the challenge of resolving these issues and balancing what was best for the parent companies in the short-term and what was best for the JV in the long-term. Macklin wanted reimbursement for faulty caps, which would have a significant impact on the profit objectives that both parent companies expected the JV to meet. The general manager had to find a solution that would satisfy both parent companies while minimizing negative impacts on the JV's results.

Selected Bibliography

Ainuddin, R. A., Beamish, P. W., Hulland, J., & Rouse, M. (2007). Resource attributes and international joint venture performance. *Journal of World Business, 42*(1), 47–60.

Arregle, J-L., Beamish, P. W., & Hebert, L. (in press). The regional dimension of MNEs' foreign subsidiary localization. *Journal of International Business Studies.*

Bartlett, C., Ghoshal, S., & Beamish, P. W. (2008). *Transnational management: Text and cases,* (5th ed.). Burr Ridge, IL: McGraw-Hill.

Beamish, P. W. (2003). The design and management of international joint ventures. In P. W. Beamish, A. Morrison, A. Inkpen and P. Rosenzweig (Eds.), *International management: Text and cases* (5th ed., pp. 120–139). Burr Ridge, IL: Irwin McGraw-Hill.

Beamish, P. W. (2001). Global strategic alliances. In *The International Encyclopedia of Business and Management* (2nd ed., pp. 2317–2335). London: International Thomson Business Press.

Beamish, P. W. (1999). The role of alliances in international entrepreneurship. In R. Wright (Ed.) *International entrepreneurship: Globalization of emerging businesses* (pp. 43–61). Greenwich, CT: JAI Press.

Beamish, P. W. (Ed.). (1998). *Strategic alliances,* Cheltenham, UK: Edward Elgar.

Beamish, P. W. (1998). Equity joint ventures in China: Compensation and motivation. *Ivey Business Quarterly, 63*(1), 67–68.

Beamish, P. W. (1994). Joint ventures in LDCs: Partner selection and performance. *Management International Review Special Issue, 34*(2), 60–74.

Beamish, P. W. (1993). The characteristics of joint ventures in the People's Republic of China. *Journal of International Marketing, 1*(2), 29–48.

Beamish, P. W. (1988). *Multinational joint ventures in developing countries.* London: Routledge.

Beamish, P. W. (1985). The characteristics of joint ventures in developed and developing countries. *Columbia Journal of World Business, 20*(3), 13–19.

Beamish, P. W., & Banks, J. C. (1987). Equity joint ventures and the theory of the multinational enterprise. *Journal of International Business Studies, 18*(2), 1–16.

Beamish, P. W., & Berdrow, I. (2003). Learning from IJVs: The unintended outcome. *Long Range Planning, 36*(3), 285–303.

Beamish, P. W., Delios, A., & Lecraw, D. J. (1997). *Japanese multinationals in the global economy.* Cheltenham, UK: Edward Elgar.

Beamish, P. W., Delios, A., & Makino, S. (2001). *Japanese subsidiaries in the new global economy.* Cheltenham, UK: Edward Elgar.

Beamish, P. W., & Inkpen, A. C. (1995). Keeping international joint ventures stable and profitable. *Long Range Planning, 28*(3), 26–36.

Beamish, P. W., & Jiang, R. (2002). Investing profitably in China: Is it getting harder? *Long Range Planning, 35*(2), 135–151.

Beamish, P. W., & Jung, J. (2005). The performance and survival of joint ventures with parents of asymmetric size. *International Management, 10*(1), 19–30.

Beamish, P. W., & Kachra, A. (2004). Number of partners and JV performance. *Journal of World Business, 39*(2), 107–120.

Beamish, P. W., & Killing, J. P. (Eds.). (1997). *Cooperative strategies: European perspectives.* San Francisco: The New Lexington Press.

Beamish, P. W., & Killing, J. P. (Eds.). (1997). *Cooperative strategies: North American perspectives.* San Francisco: The New Lexington Press.

Beamish, P. W., & Killing, J. P. (Eds.). (1997). *Cooperative strategies: Asian Pacific perspectives.* San Francisco: The New Lexington Press.

Beamish, P. W., & Lee, C. (2003). The characteristics and performance of affiliates of small and medium size multinational enterprises in an emerging market. *Journal of International Entrepreneurship, 1*(1), 121–134.

Berdrow, I., & Lane, H. (2003). International joint ventures: Creating value through successful knowledge management. *Journal of World Business, 38*(1), 15–30.

Brouthers, K. D., Brouthers, L., & Werner, S. (2003). Transaction cost enhanced entry mode choices and firm performance. *Strategic Management Journal, 24*(12), 1239–1248.

Calof, J., & Beamish, P. W. (1994). The right attitude for international success. *Business Quarterly, 59*(1), Autumn, 105–110.

Choi, C., & Beamish, P. W. (2004). Split management control and international joint venture performance. *Journal of International Business Studies, 35*(3), 201–215.

Contractor, F. J., & Lorange, P. (Eds.). (1988). *Cooperative strategies in international business.* Lexington, MA: Lexington Books.

Currall, S. C., & Inkpen, A. C. (2002). A multilevel approach to trust in joint ventures. *Journal of International Business Studies, 33*(3), 479–495.

Delios, A., & Beamish, P. W. (2004). Joint venture performance revisited: Japanese foreign subsidiaries worldwide. *Management International Review, 44*(1), 69–91.

Delios, A., & Beamish, P. W. (1999). Ownership strategy of Japanese firms: Transactional, institutional and experience influences. *Strategic Management Journal, 20*(10), 915–933.

Dhanaraj, C., & Beamish, P. W. (2004). Effect of equity ownership on the survival of international joint ventures. *Strategic Management Journal, 25*(3), 295–305.

Doz, Y. L., & Hamel, G. (1998). *Alliance advantage.* Boston: Harvard Business School Press.

Fey, C., & Beamish, P. W. (2001). Organizational climate similarity and performance: International joint ventures in Russia. *Organization Studies, 22*(5), 853–882.

Fey, C., & Beamish, P. W. (1999). Strategies for managing Russian-International joint venture conflict. *European Management Journal, 17*(1), 99–106.

Franko, L. G. (1971). *JV survival in multinational corporations.* New York: Praeger Publishers.

Geringer, J. M., & Hebert, L. (1991). Measuring performance of international joint ventures. *Journal of International Business Studies, 22*(2), 249–263.

Geringer, J. M., & Hebert, L. (1989). Control and performance of international joint ventures. *Journal of International Business Studies, 20*(2), 235–254.

Goerzen, A., & Beamish, P. W. (2005). The effect of alliance network diversity on MNE performance. *Strategic Management Journal, 26*(4), 333–354.

Gomes-Casseres, B. (1996). *The alliance revolution: The new shape of business rivalry.* Cambridge, MA: Harvard University Press.

Hannan, M. T., & Freeman, J. (1989). *Organizational ecology.* Cambridge, MA: Harvard University Press.

Harrigan, K. R. (1985). *Strategies for joint ventures.* Lexington, MA: Lexington Books.

Hébert, L., & Beamish, P. W. (2001). Control structures and performance: A comparison of international and domestic joint ventures. In K. Newman & M. Gannon (Eds.) *Handbook of cross cultural management.* Blackwell Publishers.

Hu, M. Y., & Chen, H. (1996). An empirical analysis of factors explaining foreign JV performance in China. *Journal of Business Research, 35,* 165–173.

Hymer, S. H. (1960). *The international operations of national firms: A study of direct foreign investment.* Cambridge, MA: MIT Press.

Inkpen, A. C. (2000). Learning through joint ventures: A framework of knowledge acquisition. *Journal of Management Studies, 37*(7), 1019–1043.

Inkpen, A. C., & Beamish, P. W. (1997). Knowledge, bargaining power and the instability of international joint ventures. *Academy of Management Review, 22*(1), 177–202.

Inkpen, A. C., & Crossan, M. M. (1995). Believing is seeing: Joint ventures and organizational learning. *Journal of Management Studies, 32*(5), 595–618.

Inkpen, A. C., & Currall, S. C. (2004). The co-evolution of trust, control, and learning in joint ventures. *Organization Science, 15*(5), 586–599.

Kelly, M., Schaan, J.-L., & Joncas, H. (2000). Collaboration between technology entrepreneurs and large corporations: Key design and management issues. *Journal of Small Business Strategy, 11*(2), 60–76.

Killing, J. P. (1983). *Strategies for joint venture success.* New York: Praeger.

Lane, H. W., & Beamish, P. W. (1990). Cross-cultural cooperative behavior in joint ventures in LDCs. *Management International Review, 30*(Special Issue), 87–102.

Lee, C., & Beamish, P. W. (1995). The characteristics and performance of Korean joint ventures in LDCs. *Journal of International Business Studies, 26*(3), 637–654.

Lu, J., & Beamish, P. W. (2006). Partnering strategies and performance of SMEs' international joint ventures. *Journal of Business Venturing, 21*(4), 27–48.

Luo, Y. (1995). Business strategy, market structure, and performance of international JVs: The case of JVs in China. *Management International Review, 35*(3), 241–264.

Lyles, M., & Baird, I. S. (1994). Performance of international joint ventures in two eastern European countries. *Management International Review, 34*(4), 313–330.

McLellan, K., Marcolin, B., & Beamish, P. W. (1995). The financial and strategic motivations behind IS outsourcing. *Journal of Information Technology, 10*(4), 299–321.

Makino, S., & Beamish, P. W. (1999). Matching strategy with ownership structure in Japanese joint ventures. *Academy of Management Executive, 13*(4), 17–28.

Makino, S., & Beamish, P. W. (1998). Local ownership restrictions, entry mode choice, and FDI performance: Japanese overseas subsidiaries in Asia. Special Issue on Government-Business Relations in Asia. *Asia Pacific Journal of Management, 15*(2), 119–136.

Makino, S., & Beamish, P. W. (1998). Performance and survival of joint ventures with non-conventional ownership structures. *Journal of International Business Studies, 29*(4), 797–818.

Makino, S., Chan, C. M., Isobe, T., & Beamish, P. W. (2007). Intended and unintended termination of international joint ventures. *Strategic Management Journal, 28*(11), 1113–1132.

Makino, S., & Neupert, K. E. (2000). National culture, transaction costs, and the choice between joint venture and wholly owned subsidiary. *Journal of International Business Studies, 31*(4), 705–713.

Neupert, K., & Beamish, P. W. (2001). Implementing product development alliances. *International Journal of Entrepreneurship and Innovation Management, 1*(3/4), 425–443.

Park, S. H., & Russo, M. V. (1996). When competition eclipses cooperation: An event history analysis of JV failure. *Management Science, 42,* 875–890.

Parkhe, A. (1993). Partner nationality and the structure–performance relationship in strategic alliances. *Organization Science,* 302–324.

Reiter, B. J., & Shishler, M. A. (1999). *Joint ventures: Legal and business perspectives.* Toronto: Irwin Law.

Schaan, J-L. (1988). How to control a joint venture even as a minority partner. *Journal of General Management, 14*(1), 4–16.

Schaan, J.-L., & Beamish, P. W. (1988). Joint venture general managers in developing countries. In F. Contractor & P. Lorange (Eds.), *Cooperative strategies in international business* (pp. 279–299). Lexington, MA: Lexington Books.

Stevens, D., & Beamish, P. W. (1993). Forging alliances in Mexico. *Business Quarterly, 58*(2), 79–84.

Stinchcombe, A. L. (1965). Social structure and organizations. In J. G. March (Ed.) *Handbook of organizations* (pp. 153–193). Chicago: Rand McNally.

Wilkinson, T., Peng, G. Z., Brouthers, L., & Beamish, P. W. (2008). The diminishing effect of cultural distance on subsidiary control. *Journal of International Management, 14*(2), 93–107.

Woodcock, P. C., Beamish, P. W., & Makino, S. (1994). Ownership-based entry mode strategies and international performance. *Journal of International Business Studies, 25*(2), 253–273.

Made in the USA
Lexington, KY
16 September 2017